The World of Jekyll & Hyde

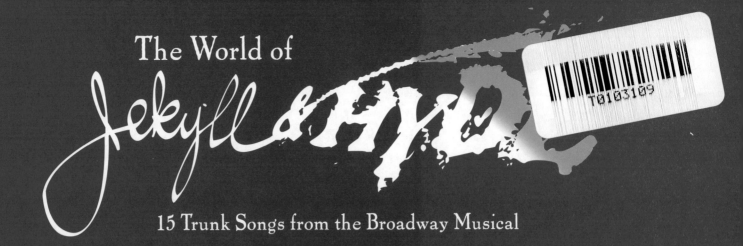

15 Trunk Songs from the Broadway Musical

Conceived for the Stage by Steve Cuden and Frank Wildhorn

Music by Frank Wildhorn

Book and Lyrics by Leslie Bricusse

ISBN 1-57560-338-1

Visit our website at www.cherrylane.com

Jekyll & Hyde

Musikalen

Scandinavian
production of
Jekyll & Hyd

CONTENTS

The World of Jekyll & Hyde

by Leslie Bricusse
Librettist and Lyricist

I was introduced to Frank Wildhorn on March 8, 1988. Our first musical collaboration, *Jekyll & Hyde*, opened on Broadway on April 28, 1997—nine years and change later.

To adapt Robert Louis Stevenson's remarkable 1886 novella into a stage musical had been Frank's dream since his college days at the University of Southern California—an idea so terrific and yet so obvious that I marveled no one had ever thought of it before. Maybe they had, but it had certainly never got as far as the stage—and most certainly not as far as between 44th and 46th Street, between Broadway and Eighth Avenue in New York City—the acknowledged center of the known Music Theatre Universe.

It all began in a carefree enough manner. I was instantly enamored of Frank's music—richly theatrical melodies set in an exciting contemporary style—and writing the first draft was, comparatively speaking, a walk in the park. I set to work eagerly on the book. A strong story line soon emerged, and Frank and I promptly pounced upon the powerful song opportunities it offered. Across that first summer, which now seems as long ago as the dark Victorian era in which Henry Jekyll first embarked upon his legendary exploration into the duality of man, we wrote a first draft of some 20 songs, while incorporating a substantial quantity of recitative into the play. Little did we know at that early stage that our journey was destined to be certainly longer than and almost as tortuous as Jekyll's—except that we emerged, a near-decade later, alive and with a happy ending.

The reaction to our work was immediate and encouraging. Everyone realized what Frank and I had known from Day One—that we could write pretty good songs together. The best response came from singers. We had lunch one day in London with Sammy Davis, Jr., and Liza Minnelli, and afterwards played them "This Is the Moment" and "A New Life," which they each respectively claimed as their own. A few weeks later, when we were all together in Hawaii for Christmas, they became the first singing stars to perform these songs in public.

The Broadway ball started, if not exactly rolling, at least moving perceptibly forward. There was even talk, thanks to Frank's power-plant energy and enthusiasm, of a New York production as early as the spring of 1989. Wiser heads prevailed, making it 1990. Wiser heads still proposed a regional tryout first, which is why we all found ourselves at the Alley Theatre in Houston in the early spring of 1990.

Stylishly directed by the Alley's Gregory Boyd, the show was an instantaneous success there, with the theatre-going public lapping it up, faults and all. Its run was extended three or four times across the summer, creating an immediate cult following, both for the show and its shining new star, Linda Eder.

Paradoxically, one of the biggest, most unlikely and almost insurmountable problems that Jekyll and Hyde has faced has been that from the very beginning it smelled of success. It was in fact full of flaws, as most draft shows are, but what *did* work worked *so* well that people came back to see it five, ten, and twenty times. The term "Jekkies" was coined to describe the die-hard fan club that has supported the show from that day to this. (A young lady who works for a major airline told me she had seen the show 43 times in 22 cities!)

So instead of undergoing the normal (normal?) sane-as-anything-ever-can-be-in-a-musical process of gradual rewriting and refining, we were pounced on by a bevy of check waving, wanna-be entrepreneurs, most of whose "Broadway" producing experience was at best a nodding acquaintance with the legit box office grosses in *Variety*. Because of Jekyll & Hyde's sensational audience response, these almost Runyonesque characters were swift to sniff our dollar potential. They started to pull *Jekyll & Hyde* in 14 different directions at once, like a litter of puppies attacking a rug, in their fevered attempts to get a piece of what they sensed would be the action.

The problem was accentuated by the fact that the ever-resourceful Frank had parlayed RCA Records in *London*—God knows how!—into making a major concept album of our first draft score, starring Colm Wilkinson of *Les Misérables* and *Phantom of the Opera* fame, as Jekyll and Hyde, in tandem with our treasured leading lady, Linda Eder. The record, too, was an instant success. It sold amazingly well for an unknown show, and the songs started to be performed on radio and television—especially "This Is the Moment," which overnight seemed to become the anthem for every form of televised competition from Miss America to the Winter Olympics to the Super Bowl to the World Series. Its notoriety became almost embarrassing, with theatre critics relishing the cheap-shot opportunity to pick it off as "ice rink music."

All of the above factors somehow combined to lead us on to a bizarre and seemingly endless Yellow Brick Road, presided over by too many chieftains and not enough Indians, that wound its twisted way from a spectacular regional success via a wretchedly misconceived nightmare New York workshop and a mind-numbing two-year legal deadlock to a money-making but still-far-from-perfect national tour.

The highlight of this otherwise desultory half-decade came in 1994 when the irrepressible Frank convinced Atlantic Records that this was the perfect moment in time to make the *second* recording of the by now two-and-a-half hour score of our still unproduced Broadway show—this time a *double* CD concept album, which he, Frank, would produce and they, Atlantic, would release on the to-be-created Atlantic Theatre label, which they, Atlantic, would form and he, Frank, would run for them! Amazingly, and at vast expense, all this came to pass, and the resultant product went on to become an even bigger success than its RCA predecessor!

It is from these first two pre-cast recordings of *Jekyll & Hyde* that so many of our "surplus songs," including the contents of this songbook, derive. In all, Frank and I wrote about 60 songs for the show as it evolved, so there are quite a few more beyond these lying around in our respective archives—with some rather nifty items among them, I have to say.

But it is a natural part of the evolution of any Broadway show for songs to be rewritten, dropped and replaced by—hopefully—better ones. Sometimes, in retrospect, they are not better—merely different approaches to the same problems presented by the text. But little wonder that so many songwriters accumulate what are known as "trunk" songs—the musical theatre's equivalent to "the cutting-room floor."

Our Yellow Brick Road finally went full circle, and in January 1995, there we were again back in our by-now-beloved Houston, this time at the 3,000-seat Music Hall. Once again, as in a recurring dream, Houston audiences went mad for *Jekyll & Hyde*, to the show-stopping tune of millions of box-office dollars.

Finally, in 1997, in the finest tradition of Yellow Brick Roads, ours led us to the Emerald City of Broadway. Thanks to the patience and abiding faith in *Jekyll & Hyde* of our longtime supporters and now Broadway producers, the Pace Theatrical Group, from guess where?—that's right, Houston!—and Fox Theatricals from Atlanta, we at long, long last crossed over from the Yellow Brick Road to the Great White Way. We were quintuply blessed to have this production designed and directed by the remarkable talents of Robin Phillips, and starring the three most dazzling new musical theatre talents, I venture to suggest, to arrive on Broadway in many a season—Robert Cuccioli, Linda Eder, and Christine Noll.

Future productions of *Jekyll & Hyde* are already in the works for a dozen countries around the world—including Australia, Japan, Spain, Denmark, Canada, England, Italy, and the Benelux countries—and in fact the show is already running in Germany, Sweden, and Holland. In each of these productions, further refinements have seen such songs as "I Need to Know" and "Bring On the Men" return to the score, unquestionably to its benefit. They're back to stay.

And best of all—wouldn't you know?—a smiling Frank Wildhorn, having presided over the Broadway and German cast albums, is now happily contemplating the *fifth* CD of the show's score—*Jekyll & Hyde—The Symphonic Version*—to celebrate our fourth year on Broadway!

—Leslie Bricusse
Beverly Hills, CA
February 7, 2000

Jekyll & HYDE
DAS MUSICAL

German
production of
Jekyll & Hyde

About the Songs

by Frank Wildhorn

BRING ON THE MEN
This is the song most requested by our *Jekyll & Hyde* fans and the song they'd most like to see in the Broadway production. I can tell you that if Linda ever comes back to *Jekyll* on Broadway, "Bring On the Men" will come back as well.

THE GIRLS OF THE NIGHT
This is currently being performed in the international versions of *Jekyll* and it's a melody I miss in the Broadway production. On the other hand, I can't have a four-hour show, can I?

HOSPITAL BOARD
This "sung-through" version from the *Complete Works* album is also currently being performed around the world and on tour.

I NEED TO KNOW
This was the first song Anthony Warlow recorded when we did the sessions, and his vocal on it is incredible. It gave us an idea of what was to come from such a great singer.

IT'S OVER NOW
This little motif appears in various ways in various versions around the world.

LETTING GO
There are actually a few versions of "Letting Go." I think my favorite is from the 1990 show. The version that Linda and Colm did on the first *Jekyll* album was written only for the record. It's one of those titles, throughout the history of *Jekyll & Hyde*, that's gone through many versions. I bet there are fans who know more about this than I do.

LOVE HAS COME OF AGE
This song was dropped after the Houston Alley production of 1990. It has since been replaced by "Take Me As I Am." I understand this song was actually a minor hit in Australia, and I'll always remember the beautiful rendition Chuck Wagner and Rebecca Spencer did.

NO ONE MUST EVER KNOW
This is another little motif that has popped up in various forms over the years.

POSSESSED
Also a little motif that has popped up in various forms over the years.

RETRIBUTION
Hyde's musical vocabulary without words.

SEDUCTION
The first instrumental version of "Sympathy, Tenderness," which inspired Leslie to write "Sympathy, Tenderness."

TILL YOU CAME INTO MY LIFE
You would not believe how many times I hear this song at auditions, with guys coming in thinking it's one of Jekyll's big songs in the show. Maybe for the concert version . . . ?

TRANSFORMATION
Has gone through many . . .

WE STILL HAVE TIME
Colm and Linda's recording of this is wonderful, and I'm sure we'll hear it in a *Jekyll & Hyde* concert version one day.

THE WORLD HAS GONE INSANE
In the German production of *Jekyll & Hyde*, Jekyll not only sings this song, but sings it while he's flying around. Like so many other scenes in the German production, it is mind-blowing and something you have to see.

Leslie Bricusse
Composer, Lyricist, Librettist

Double Oscar and Grammy Winner Leslie Bricusse is a writer-composer-lyricist who has contributed to many musical films and plays during his career. He was born in London and educated at University College School and Gonville and Caius College, Cambridge. At Cambridge he was President of the Footlights Revue Club, and founded the Music Comedy Club. There he co-authored, directed, and performed in his first two musical shows, *Out of the Blue* and *Lady at the Wheel*, both of which made their way to London's West End. He also found time in the gaps to acquire a Master of Arts Degree.

The late, great Beatrice Lillie plucked him out of the Footlights Revue at the Phoenix Theatre and made him her leading man in *An Evening with Beatrice Lillie* at the Globe Theatre. There he spent the first year of his professional life writing another musical, *The Boy on the Corner*, and the screenplay and score of his first motion picture, *Charley Moon*, which won him his first Ivor Novello Award. That year he decided to drop the possibilities of directing and performing and concentrate his career on becoming a full-time writer-composer-lyricist.

His subsequent stage musicals include *Stop the World—I Want to Get Off*, *The Roar of the Greasepaint—The Smell of the Crowd*, *Scrooge*, *Pickwick*, *Harvey*, *The Good Old Bad Old Days*, *Goodbye Mr. Chips*, *Henry's Wives*, *Kennedy*, *Sherlock Holmes*, *Jekyll & Hyde*, and *Victor/Victoria*. He has written songs and/or screenplays for such films as *Doctor Dolittle*, *Scrooge*, *Willy Wonka and the Chocolate Factory*, *Goodbye Mr. Chips*, *Peter Pan*, *Superman*, *Victor/Victoria*, *Santa Claus—The Movie*, *Home Alone* and *Home Alone II*, *Hook*, *Tom and Jerry—The Movie*, and various *Pink Panther* films.

Bricusse has written more than 40 musical shows and films, and over the years has had the good fortune to enjoy fruitful collaborations with a wonderful array of musical talents, including Anthony Newley, Henry Mancini, John Williams, John Barry, Quincy Jones, Jerry Goldsmith, Jule Styne, André Previn, Frank Wildhorn, and Peter Ilyitch Tchaikovsky (whose *Nutcracker Suite* he has adapted into a song score).

His better-known songs include "What Kind of Fool Am I?," "Once in a Lifetime," "Gonna Build a Mountain," "Who Can I Turn To?," "The Joker," "If I Ruled the World," "My Kind of Girl," "Talk to the Animals," "You and I," "Feeling Good," "When I Look in Your Eyes," "Goldfinger," "Can You Read My Mind?" (the love theme from *Superman*), "You Only Live Twice," "Le Jazz Hot!," "On a Wonderful Day Like Today," "Two for the Road," "The Candy Man," "This Is the Moment," and "Crazy World."

He has been nominated for ten Academy Awards, nine Grammys, and four Tonys, and has won two Oscars, a Grammy, and eight Ivor Novello Awards, the premiere British music award.

Hundreds of Bricusse's songs have been recorded by major artists, including Frank Sinatra, Nat King Cole, Judy Garland, Aretha Franklin, Barbra Streisand, Sammy Davis, Jr. (who recorded 60 Bricusse songs), Tony Bennett, Shirley Bassey, Tom Jones, Petula Clark, Julie Andrews, Liza Minnelli, Andy Williams, Rex Harrison, Elaine Paige, Anthony Newley, Michael Feinstein, Bette Midler, The Moody Blues, Nancy Sinatra, Lena Horne, Sergio Mendes, Dionne Warwick, Robert Goulet, Matt Munro, Ray Charles, Ethel Merman, Placido Domingo, Jennifer Holliday, Danny Kaye, Robbie Williams and Mariah Carey.

In 1989 he received the Kennedy Award for consistent excellence in Britsh songwriting, bestowed by the British Academy of Songwriters, Composers, and Authors, and was inducted into the American Songwriters Hall of Fame in New York—only the fourth Englishman to be so honored, after Noël Coward, John Lennon, and Paul McCartney.

Bricusse is currently represented on Broadway and across the United States by *Jekyll & Hyde*, written with Frank Wildhorn and now in its fourth years at the Plymouth Theatre in New York, with nearly a dozen international productions either playing or planned in the next two years.

Another Bricusse perennial, his musical version of *Scrooge*, in which Anthony Newley starred at the Dominion Theatre in London's West End in the 1996/97 season, is also seen annually in a number of productions in the UK, Europe, the US, and Japan.

For *Doctor Dolittle*, his current new stage musical now playing in England, starring Phillips Schofield and almost one hundred assorted animatronic animals created by Jim Henson's Creature Shop, Bricusse serves as librettist, composer, lyricist and co-producer. Further productions are planned in the United States, Australia and Japan.

His next project is a remarkable musical biography of the world's greatest entertainer, the late Sammy Davis, Jr., entitled *Sammy*, written in collaboration with Quincy Jones and due for production in America in 2001. Another Bricusse solo effort, *Noah's Ark*, will open in England, also in 2001.

Frank Wildhorn's works span the worlds of popular, theatrical, and classical music.

In 1999 Mr. Wildhorn became the first American composer in 22 years to have three shows running simultaneously on Broadway—*Jekyll & Hyde* at the Plymouth Theatre, *The Scarlet Pimpernel* at the Minskoff, and *The Civil War* at the St. James Theatre, whose previews began in March '99.

The Civil War received two 1999 Tony nominations: Best New Musical and Best Score. The show's National Tour began in January 2000. Prior to its Broadway run, Wildhorn produced a star-studded double concept album of *The Civil War* (featuring Hootie & The Blowfish, Blues Traveler, Trisha Yearwood, Travis Tritt, Dr. John, and Betty Buckley among others), as well as the single album *The Nashville Sessions*.

Jekyll & Hyde holds the distinction of being the first new American musical to have two internationally released concept recordings of the score: *Highlights of Jekyll & Hyde* on RCA, and *Jekyll & Hyde — The Complete Work* on Atlantic Records. The success of this recording launched a new label, Atlantic Theatre. Songs from *Jekyll & Hyde*, such as "Someone Like You," "A New Life," and "This Is the Moment," have been performed worldwide and have been featured at the Olympics, the Super Bowl, the World Series, the WNBA Championships, Miss America Pageant, the 1996 Democratic National Convention, and the Inauguration of President Clinton (sung by Jennifer Holliday). The Broadway cast recording was released in July '97.

Frank Wildhorn
Composer, Producer

Photo by Beth Kelly

The Bremen, Germany production and the recent opening of *Jekyll & Hyde* in Sweden mark the first of the next eight international productions. Future international plans include productions in Madrid, Tokyo, Copenhagen, Helsinki, London, and Australia. The two-year American tour of *Jekyll & Hyde* began in April '99.

After a four-city tour, a new *Scarlet Pimpernel* Broadway cast has now reached their permanent home at the Neil Simon Theatre. The show's National Tour began in February 2000, and is booked for a two-year run. The score has yielded its own Top 40 AC Hit with the song "You Are My Home," a duet recorded by Peabo Bryson and Linda Eder. The Broadway cast recording was released in February '98. A new album entitled *The Scarlet Pimpernel: Encore!*, featuring Rex Smith and Rachel York, was added to the original cast album and released as a compilation in November '99.

Artists who have recorded and performed Mr. Wildhorn's music include Whitney Houston (the international number one hit "Where Do Broken Hearts Go"), Natalie Cole, Kenny Rogers, Sammy Davis, Jr., Liza Minnelli, Julie Andrews, Freddie Jackson, Peabo Bryson, Trisha Yearwood, Deana Carter, Tracy Lawrence, John Berry, Trace Adkins, Travis Tritt, Patti La Belle, Bebe Winans, Bryan White, Betty Buckley, Ben Vereen, Regina Bell, The Moody Blues, Jeffrey Osborne, Jennifer Holliday, Stacy Lattisaw, Dennis DeYoung, Molly Hatchet, Brenda Russell, John Raitt, Anthony Warlow, Stanley Turrentine, Colm Wilkinson, and Linda Eder, whose Atlantic albums *It's Time* and *It's No Secret Anymore* were written and co-produced by Wildhorn.

Mr. Wildhorn's new projects include: *Dracula*; *The Romantics*, a multi-album project in collaboration with such lyricists as Leslie Bricusse, Stephen Schwartz, Maury Yeston, and Don Black; *Wonderland*, in development with illusionist/magician David Copperfield; *Havana*, a romantic musical comedy written with Gregory Boyd and Jack Murphy; *Svengali*; the children's musical *Big Nose*; *Bonnie & Clyde*; *Camille Claudel*; *F. Scott & Zelda Fitzgerald*; and *Queen Christina*. In the classical world, Mr. Wildhorn is currently developing a full-length ballet, *Natasha*.

Mr. Wildhorn is an Associate Artist in Musical Theatre with an Endowed Chair at the Alley Theatre in Houston, where he launched *Jekyll & Hyde*, *Svengali*, and *The Civil War*. He also wrote music for Arthur Kopit's play *The Road to Nirvana*, scored the play *Cyrano de Bergerac* and wrote additional songs for Julie Andrews in Broadway's *Victor/Victoria*. Mr. Wildhorn also composed and served as musical director for the Opening Ceremonies of the 1998 Goodwill Games in New York City.

Mr. Wildhorn enjoys a long-term relationship with Warner Bros. Pictures. Under the auspices of Lauren Shuler-Donner and Dick Donner, he is developing both feature-length musical animated films and live action musical projects.

In addition, Mr. Wildhorn is Creative Director of Atlantic Theatre, a division of Atlantic Records. In this capacity, he develops new American musical works and their potential stars, as well as strengthens the relationship between commercial theatre and the music industry.

Born in New York City and raised in Florida, Frank Wildhorn now resides in North Salem, NY, with his wife and muse Linda Eder and his son Justin's baby brother, Jake.

Bring On the Men

Words by Leslie Bricusse

Music by Frank Wildhorn

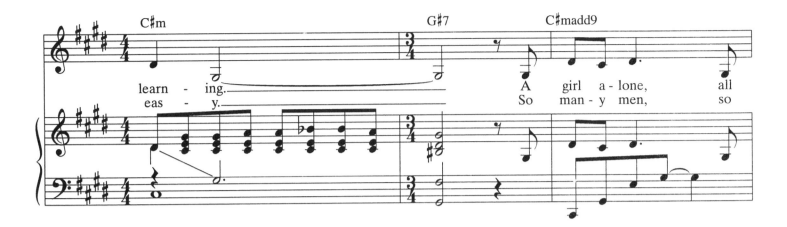

11

real - ly do, I   don't suc - ceed! So let's bring
make me sick, so God knows why we say: Bring

Bright cut time (Tempo II)

on   the men——— and let the fun be - gin;——— a lit - tle

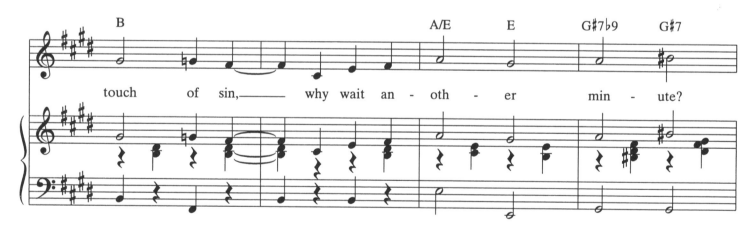

touch of sin,——— why wait an - oth - er min - ute?

Step this way;——— it's time for us to play.——— They say we

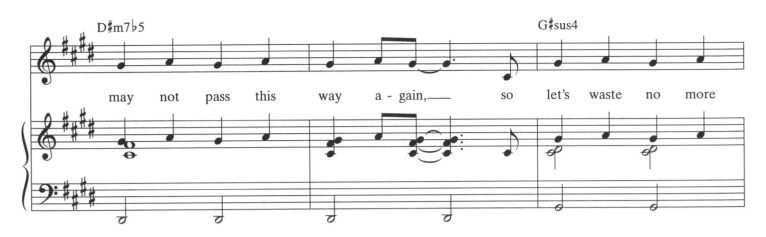

may not pass this way a - gain,____ so let's waste no more

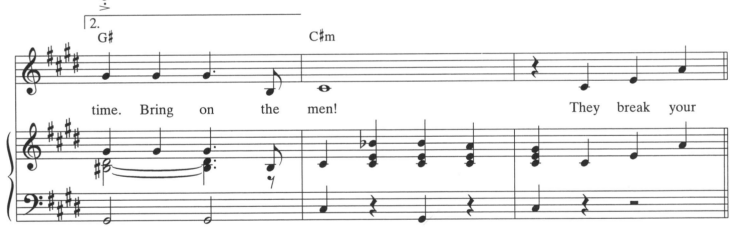

time. Bring on the men!

time. Bring on the men!   They break your

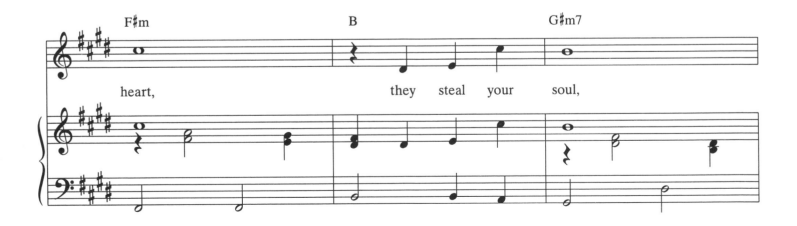

heart,   they steal your soul,

take you a - part, and yet they some - how

make you whole. So what's their game?

Slowly

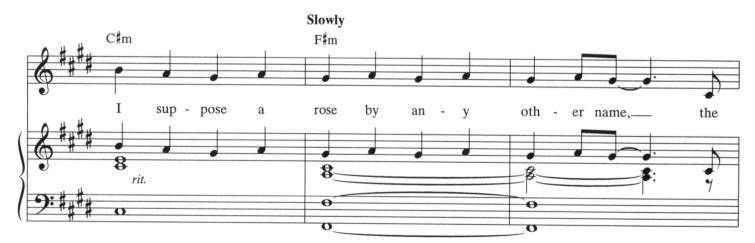

I sup - pose a rose by an - y oth - er name,___ the

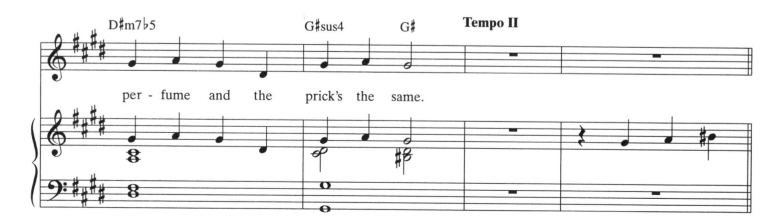

per - fume and the prick's the same.

Tempo II

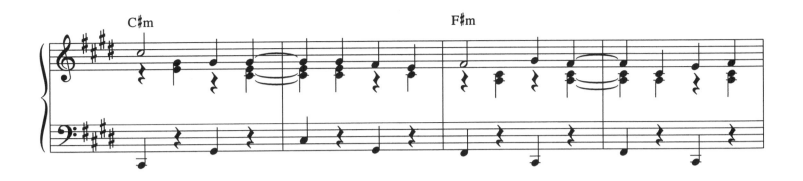

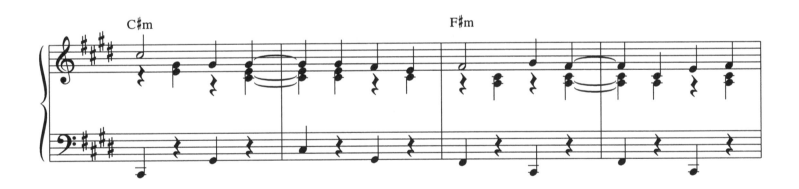

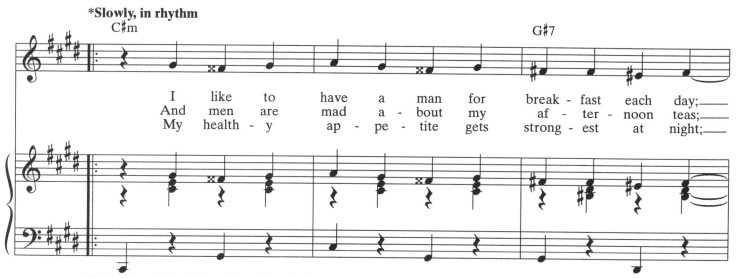

*Slowly, in rhythm

I like to have a man for break-fast each day;_____
And men are mad a-bout my af-ter-noon teas;_____
My health-y ap-pe-tite gets strong-est at night;_____

* This section is played three times: Slow, Moderately, and Fast (Tempo II).

I'm ver - y so - cial and I
they're quite in - for - mal, I just
my at home din - ners are my

like it that way._____
do it to please._____
men friends' de - light._____

By late mid - le
Those trip - le
When I in -

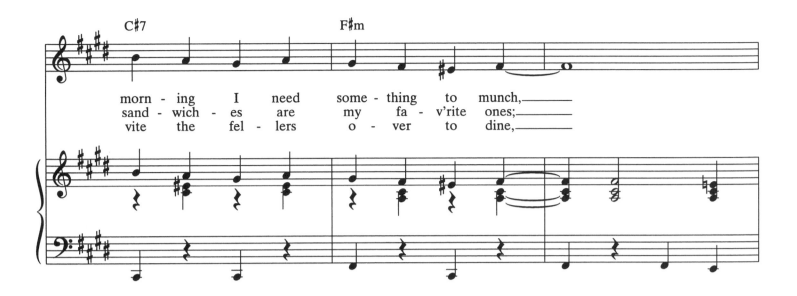

morn - ing   I   need   some - thing   to   munch,———
sand - wich - es   are   my   fa - v'rite   ones;———
vite   the   fel - lers   o - ver   to   dine,———

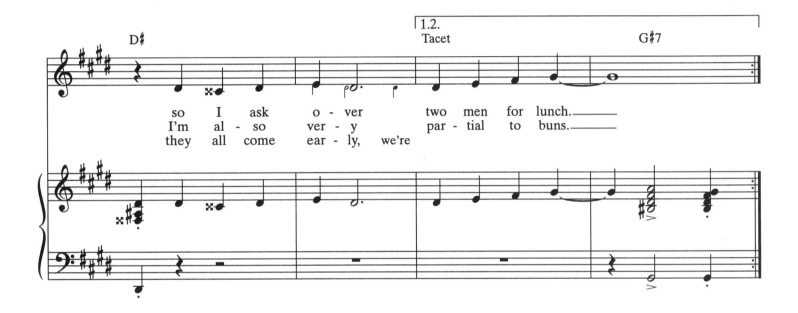

so   I   ask   o - ver   two   men   for   lunch.———
I'm   al - so   ver - y   par - tial   to   buns.———
they   all   come   ear - ly,   we're

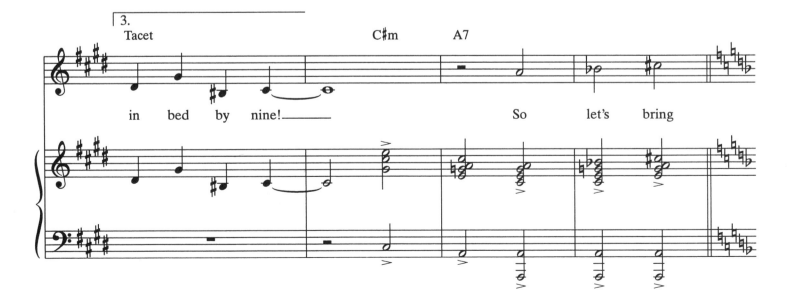

in   bed   by   nine!———   So   let's   bring

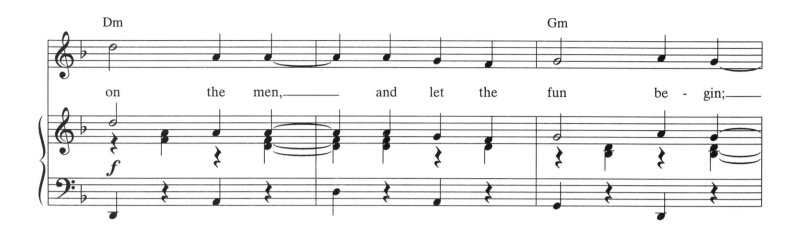

on the men,_____ and let the fun be - gin;_____

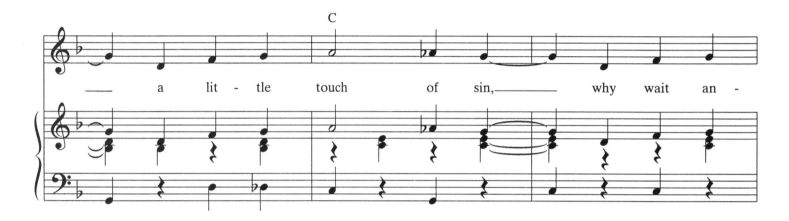

_____ a lit - tle touch of sin,_____ why wait an -

oth - er min - ute? Step this way,_____

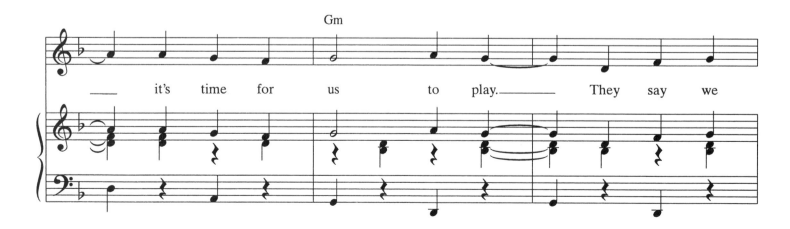

_____ it's time for us to play._____ They say we

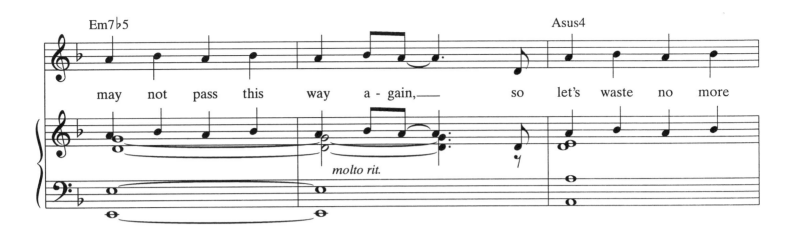

may not pass this way a - gain,_____ so let's waste no more

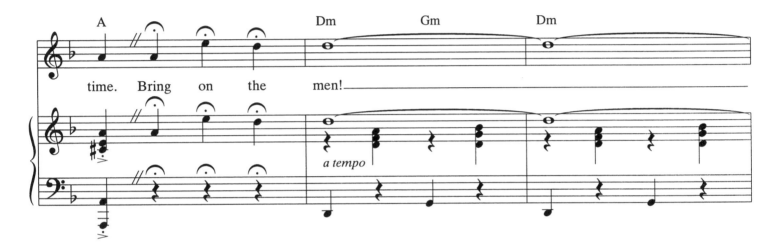

time. Bring on the men!_____

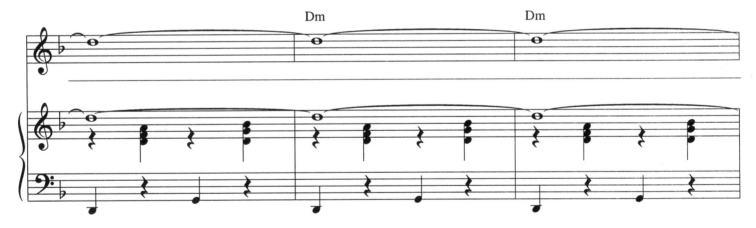

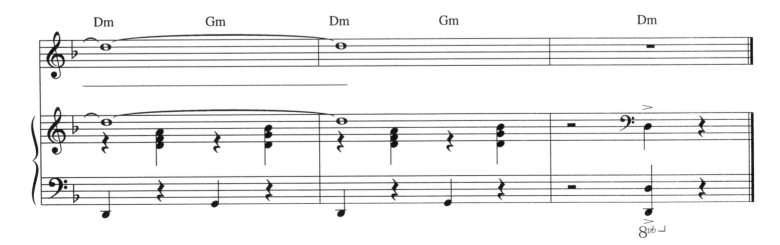

The Girls of the Night

Words by Leslie Bricusse

Music by Frank Wildhorn

Moderately, flowing

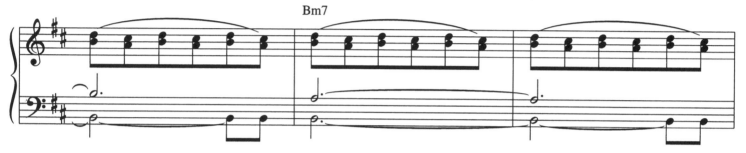

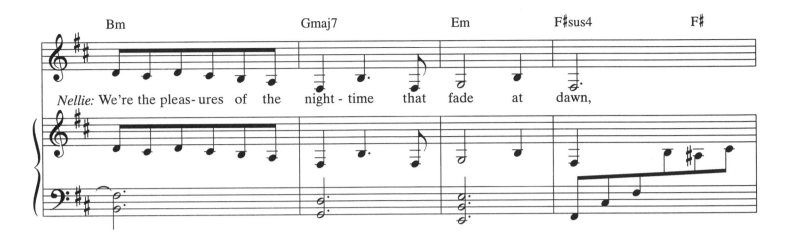

Nellie: We're the pleas- ures of the night - time that fade at dawn,

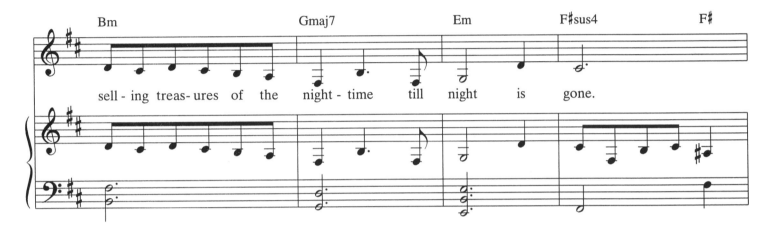

sell - ing treas- ures of the night - time till night is gone.

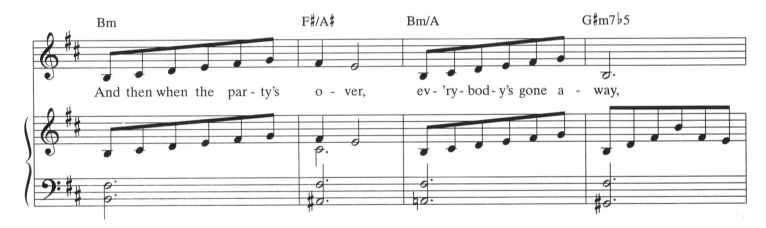

And then when the par - ty's o - ver, ev - 'ry - bod - y's gone a - way,

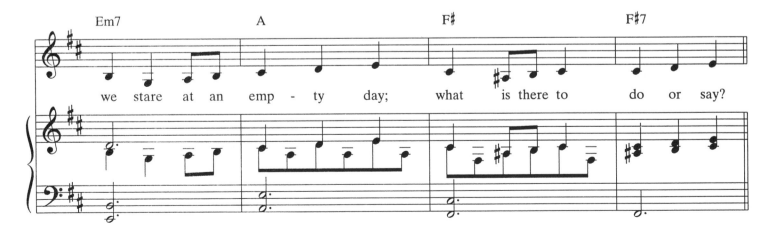

we stare at an emp - ty day; what is there to do or say?

Night - time is where we live; night is when we give ev - 'ry - thing we

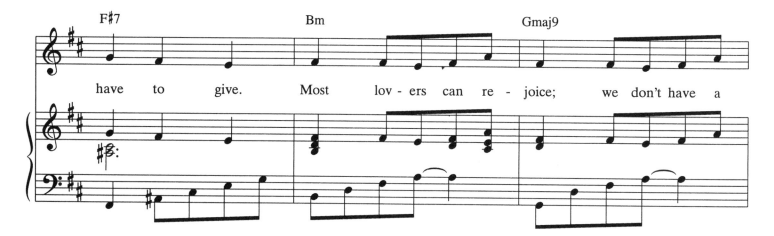

have to give. Most lov - ers can re - joice; we don't have a

choice; we just know we have to give._____ That's why the day can

nev - er be bright for the girls of the night._____

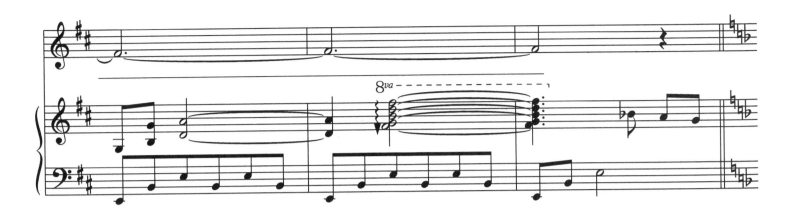

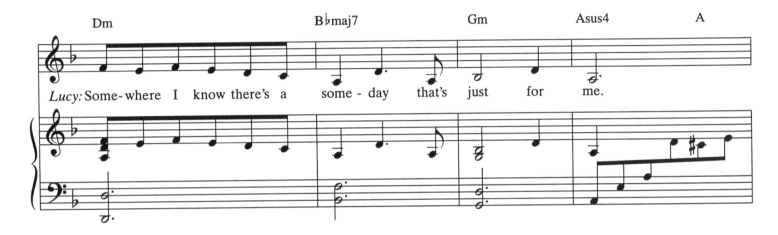

Lucy: Some-where I know there's a some - day that's just for me.

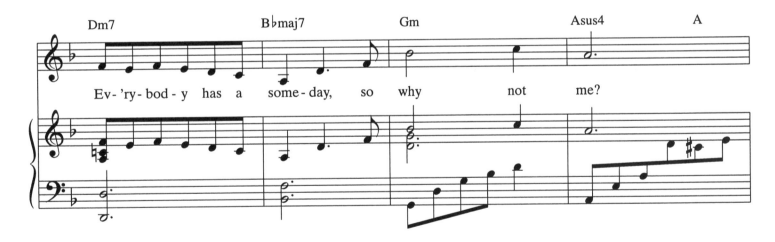

Ev-'ry-bod-y has a some - day, so why not me?

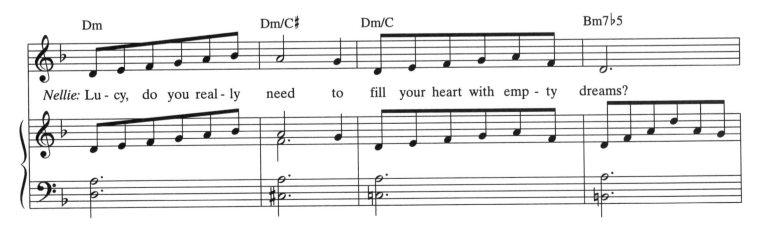

Nellie: Lu - cy, do you real - ly need to fill your heart with emp - ty dreams?

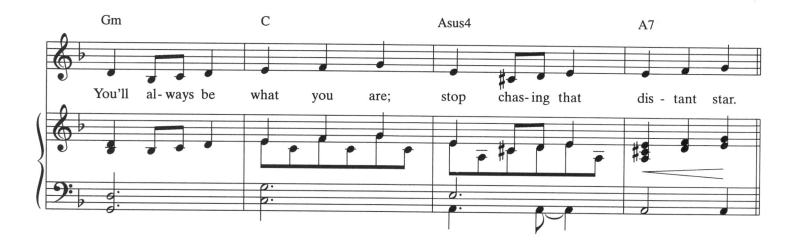

You'll al-ways be what you are; stop chas-ing that dis - tant star.

Both: Night - time is where we live; night is when we give ev - 'ry-thing we

have to give. Most lov - ers can re - joice; we don't have a

choice; we just know we have to give. That's why the day can nev - er be

bright for the girls of the night.

Lucy: Fly a - way, fly a - way; let me find my wings.

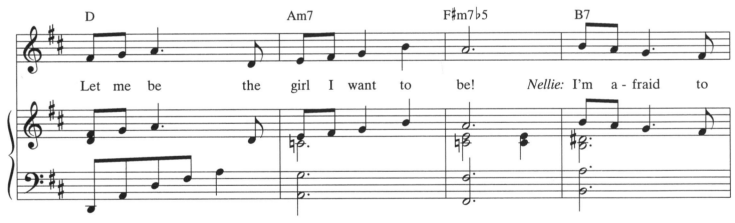

Let me be the girl I want to be! *Nellie:* I'm a - fraid to

fly a - way, for all I have is here. *Lucy:* I

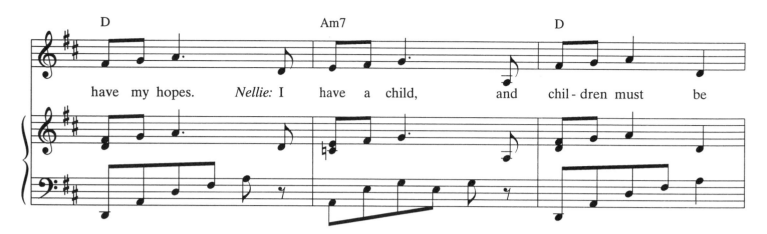

have my hopes. *Nellie:* I have a child, and chil-dren must be

fed. For - get your hopes, or you will be mis - led.

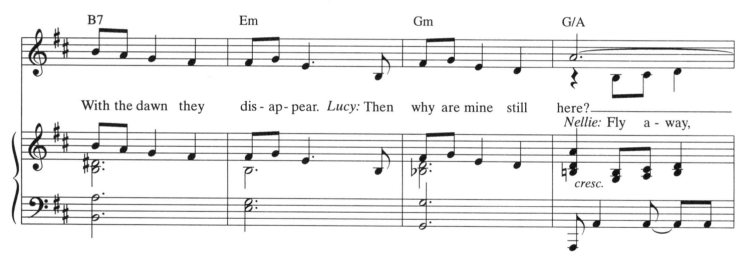

With the dawn they dis - ap-pear. *Lucy:* Then why are mine still here?_____ *Nellie:* Fly a - way,

fly a - way, fly a - way._____

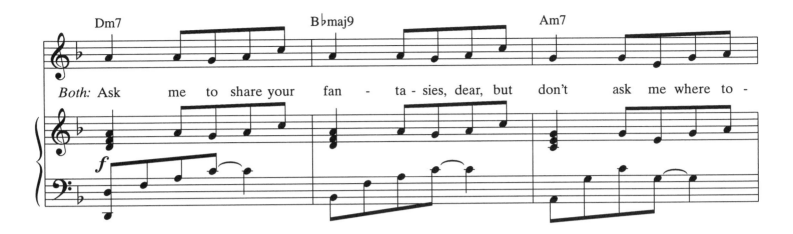

Both: Ask me to share your fan - ta - sies, dear, but don't ask me where to -

mor - row is. Don't ask me where to find hap - pi - ness, though

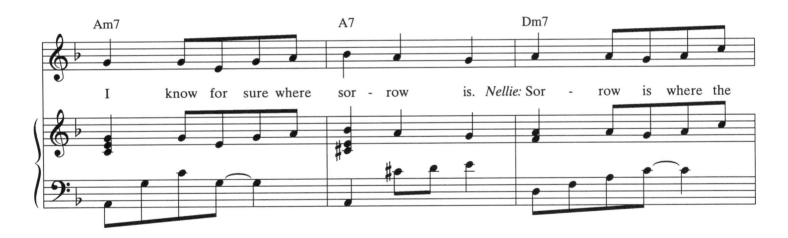

I know for sure where sor - row is. *Nellie:* Sor - row is where the

dark meets the light.

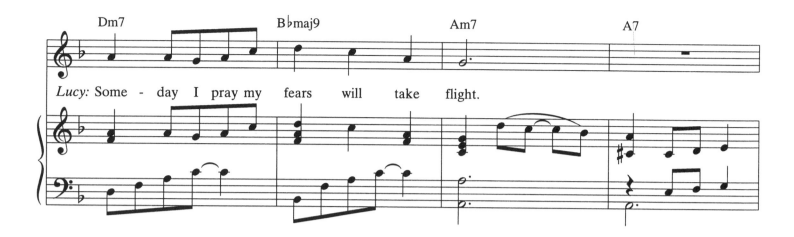

Lucy: Some - day I pray my fears will take flight.

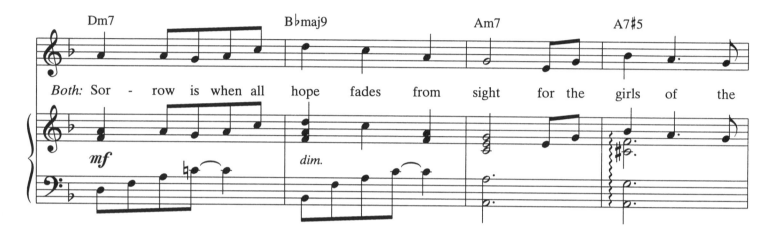

Both: Sor - row is when all hope fades from sight for the girls of the

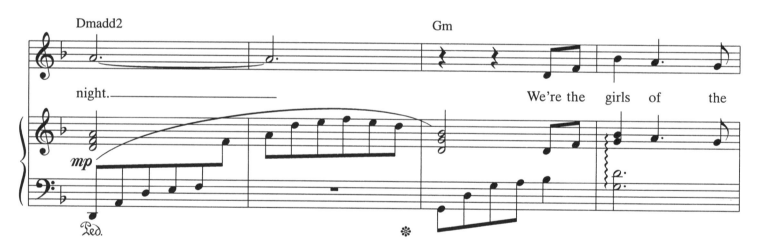

night._____ We're the girls of the

night,_____ just the girls of the night.

Hospital Board

Words by Steve Cuden,
Leslie Bricusse and Frank Wildhorn

Music by Frank Wildhorn

Moderately

Friends, you're a-ware there are two sides to each of us,

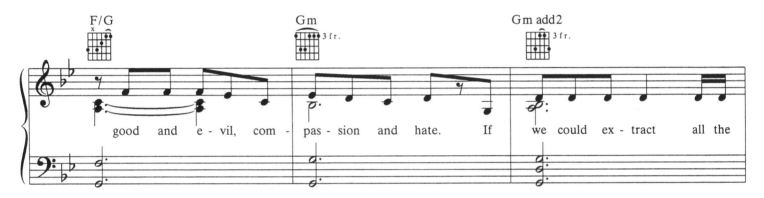

good and e-vil, com-pas-sion and hate. If we could ex-tract all the

e-vil from each of us, think of the world___ that we could cre-ate. A

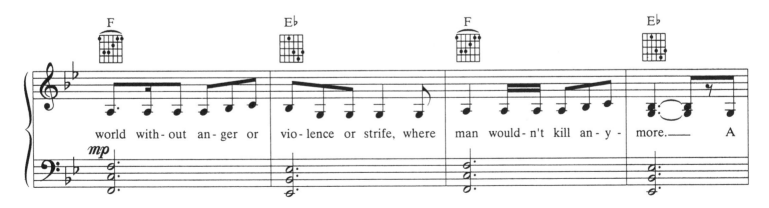

world with-out an-ger or vio-lence or strife, where man would-n't kill an-y-more.___ A

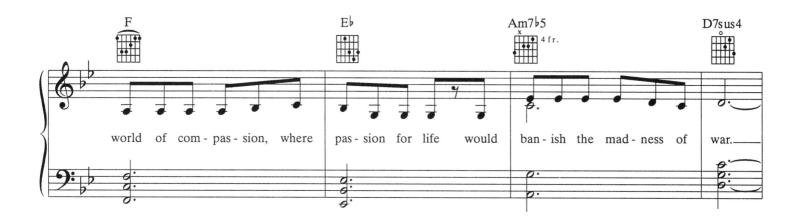

world of com-pas-sion, where pas-sion for life would ban-ish the mad-ness of war.

I have de-vel-oped in ac-tu'l re-al-i-ty, chem-i-cal for-mu-lae

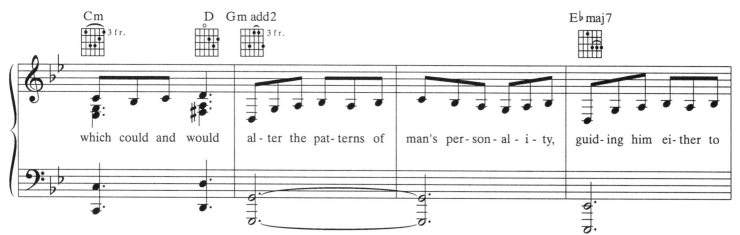

which could and would al-ter the pat-terns of man's per-son-al-i-ty, guid-ing him ei-ther to

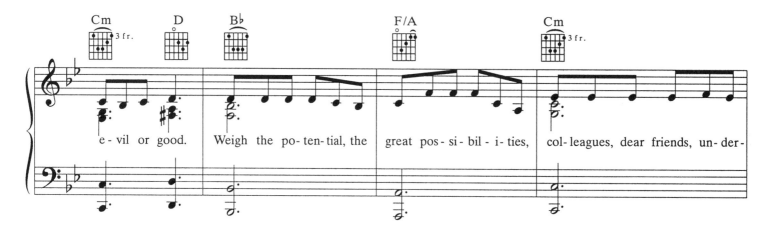

e-vil or good. Weigh the po-ten-tial, the great pos-si-bil-i-ties, col-leagues, dear friends, un-der-

stand   we have a chance to make   his-to-ry here in our   hand.

Here is a chance to take   charge of our fate, deep   down you must know that to-

mor-row's too late.   One rule of life we can-not re-ar-range, the   on-ly thing con-stant is

change,   the on-ly thing con-stant is   *change.*

I Need to Know

Words by Leslie Bricusse

Music by Frank Wildhorn

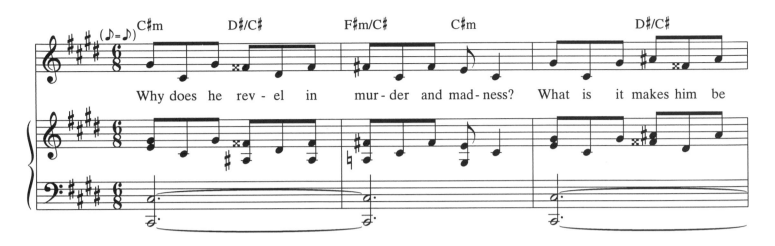

Why does he rev-el in mur-der and mad-ness? What is it makes him be

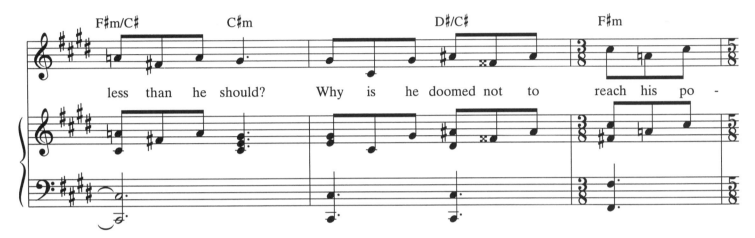

less than he should? Why is he doomed not to reach his po-

ten-tial?_____ His soul is black when he turns his back up-on

Moderately, in rhythm

good._____

I

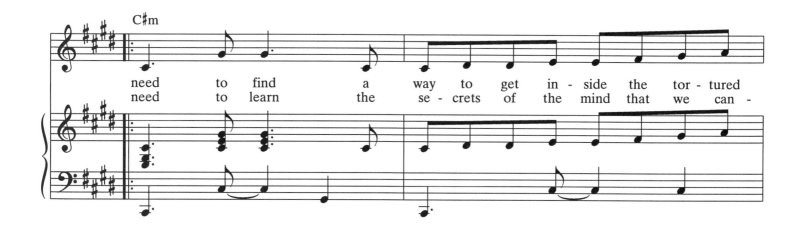

need to find a way to get in-side the tor-tured
need to learn the se-crets of the mind that we can-

mind of man. I need to try to
not dis-cern. I need to learn to the

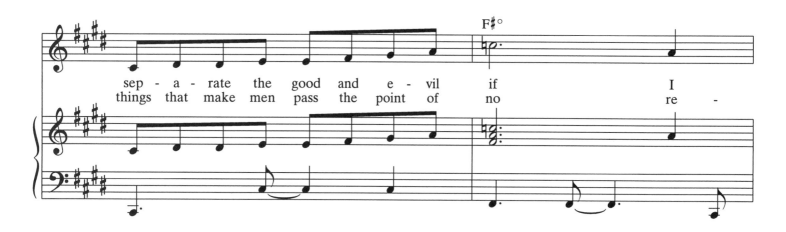

sep-a-rate the good and e-vil if I
things that make men pass the point of no re-

can. One thing is cer-tain, the e-vil is strong-er;
turn. Why does a wise man take leave of his sens-es?

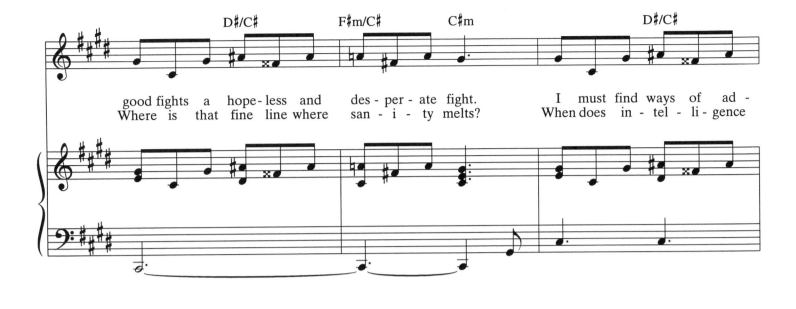

good fights a hope-less and des-per-ate fight.   I must find ways of ad -
Where is that fine line where san - i - ty melts?   When does in - tel - li - gence

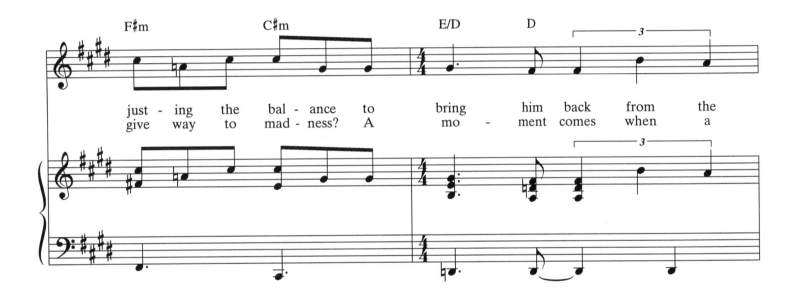

just - ing the bal - ance to   bring him back from the
give way to mad - ness?   A mo - ment comes from when a

emp - ty black edge of   night._____ I need to
man be - comes some - thing else...._____ I need to

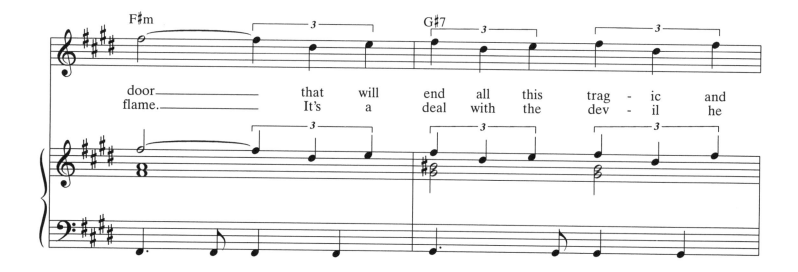

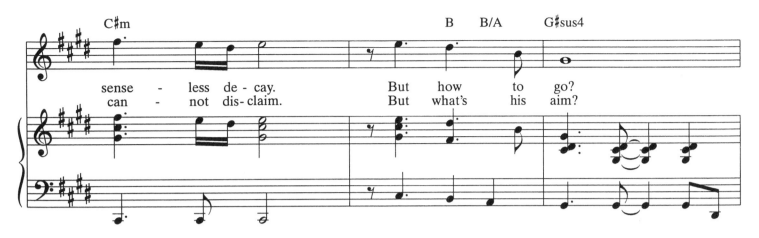

C#m   B B/A G#sus4

sense - less de - cay.   But how to go?
can - not dis- claim.   But what's his aim?

G#   **1.** C#m

I need to know!   I
I need to

dim.

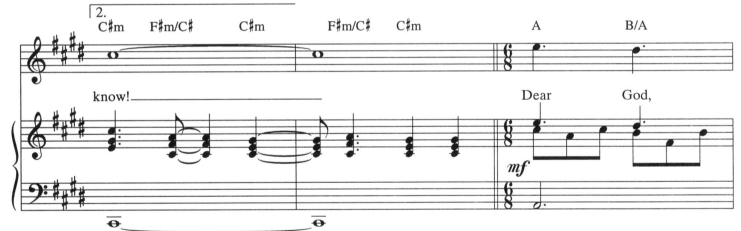

2.
C#m F#m/C# C#m   F#m/C# C#m   A   B/A

know!   Dear God,

mf

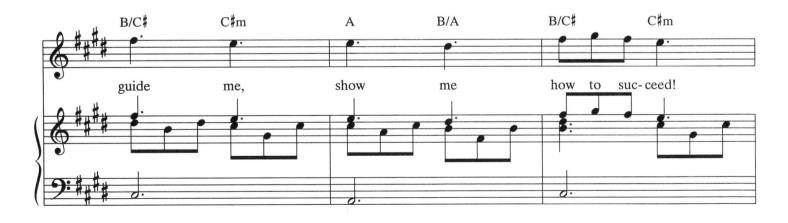

B/C#   C#m   A   B/A   B/C#   C#m

guide me, show me how to suc- ceed!

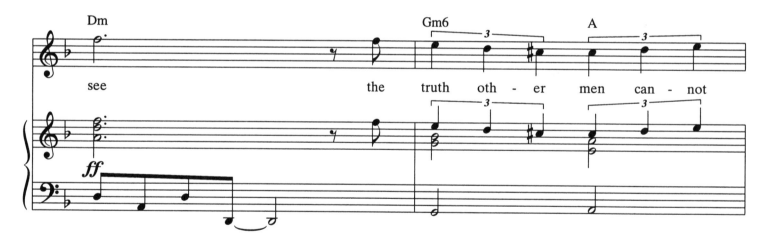

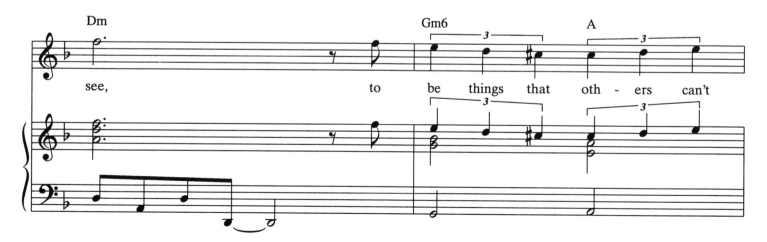

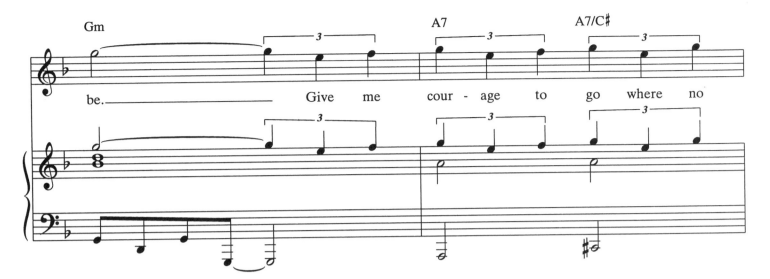

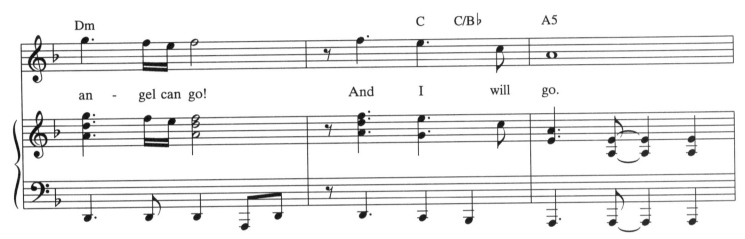

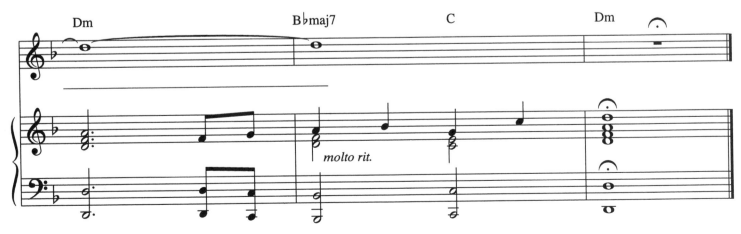

It's Over Now

Words by
Leslie Bricusse and Frank Wildhorn

Music by Frank Wildhorn

Moderately slow

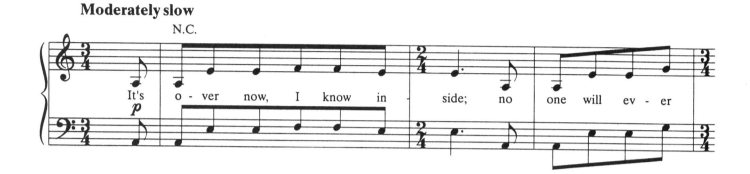

It's o - ver now, I know in - side; no one will ev - er

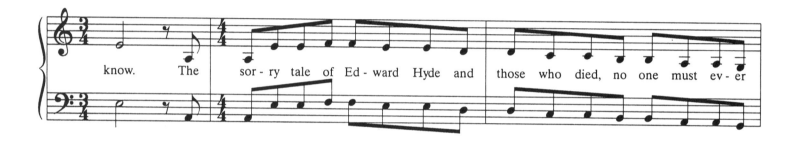

know. The sor - ry tale of Ed - ward Hyde and those who died, no one must ev - er

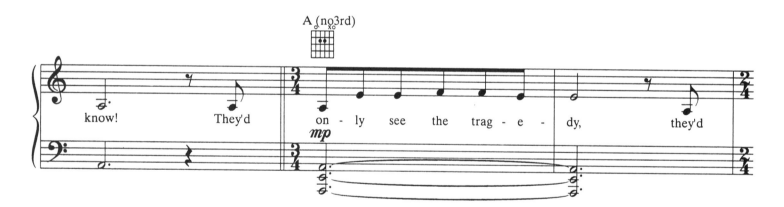

know! They'd on - ly see the trag - e - dy, they'd

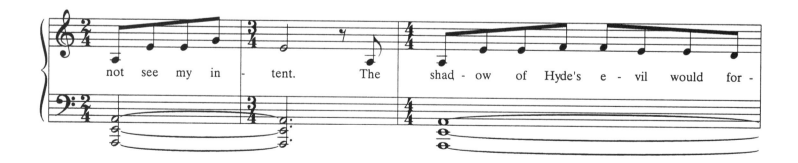

not see my in - tent. The shad - ow of Hyde's e - vil would for -

ev - er kill the good that I had meant._____

A (no3rd)

Am I a good man? Am I a

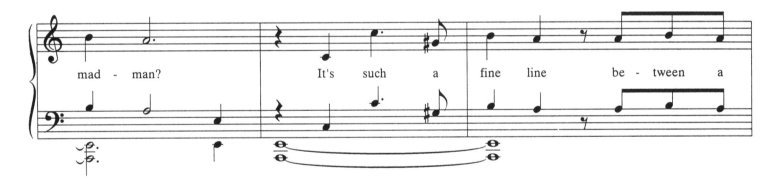

mad - man? It's such a fine line be - tween a

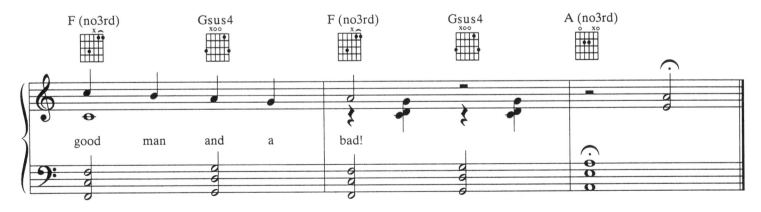

F (no3rd) Gsus4 F (no3rd) Gsus4 A (no3rd)

good man and a bad!

Letting Go

Words by Leslie Bricusse

Music by Frank Wildhorn

bye to you, it's the last thing in life I'll ev - er
time to part; giv - ing way to the day that may well

want to do. I know it has to be, but it's so
break my heart. It's not a thing I choose; to win I

1.
hard for me. Let - ting

2.
have to lose. *Lisa:* Let - ting

go, mov - ing on in my life in - to the time to come. Day by

day,   page by page,   sure of what I've be-come.   But then you

al - ways knew   that's what I had to do.   *Both:* For I

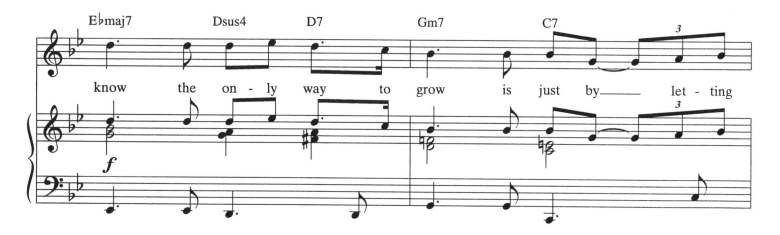

know   the on - ly way to grow   is just by___ let - ting

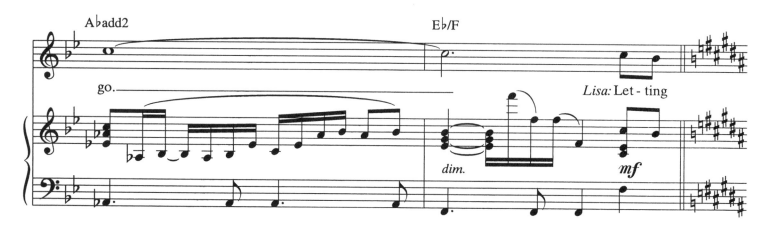

go.___   *Lisa:* Let - ting

go;   when the time comes I know I shall re-

turn some - day. But till then, this is when I have to

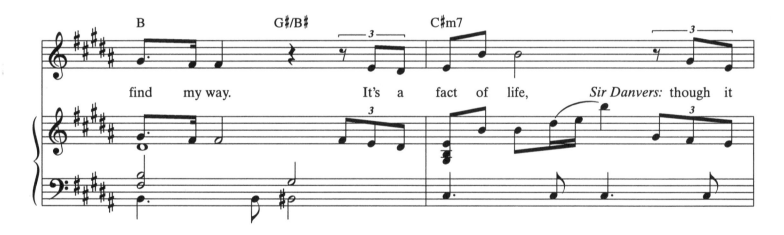

find my way. It's a fact of life, *Sir Danvers:* though it

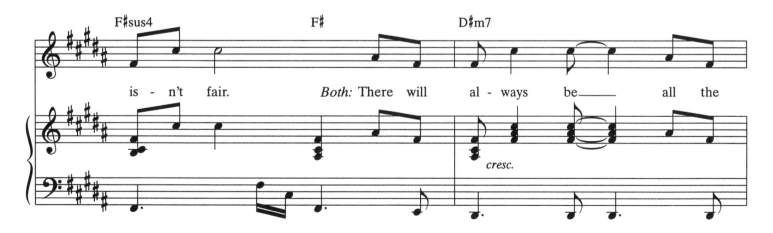

is - n't fair. *Both:* There will al - ways be___ all the

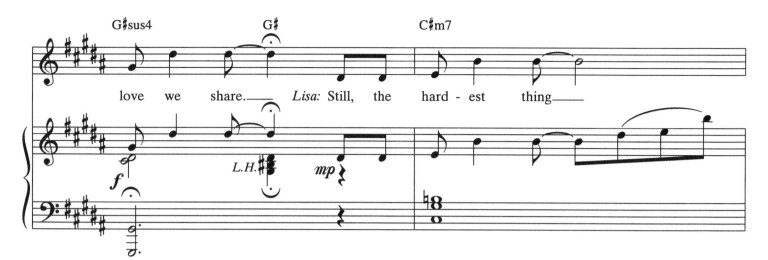

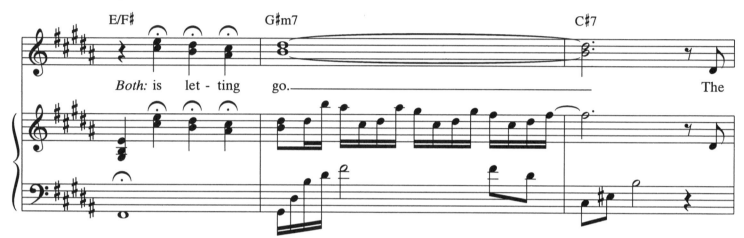

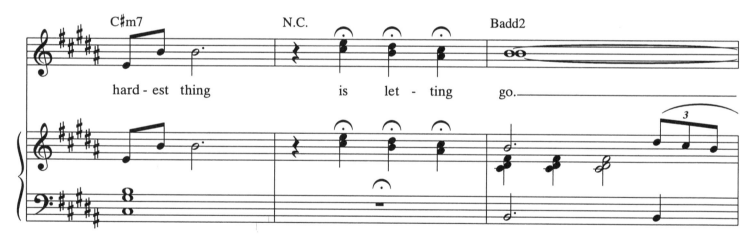

Love Has Come of Age

Words by
Leslie Bricusse and Frank Wildhorn

Music by Frank Wildhorn

Moderately slow

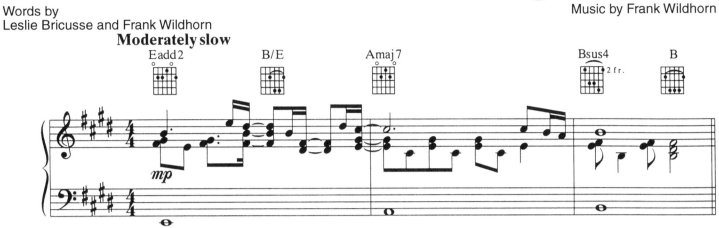

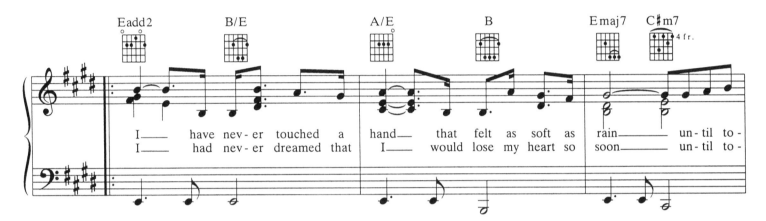

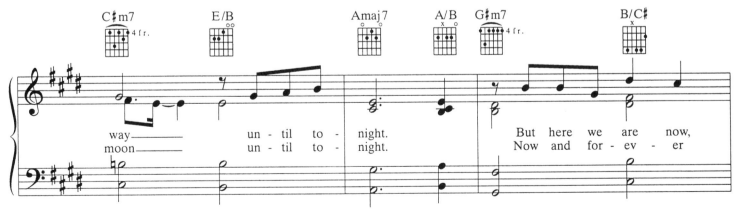

No One Must Ever Know

Words by Steve Cuden,
Leslie Bricusse and Frank Wildhorn

Music by Frank Wildhorn

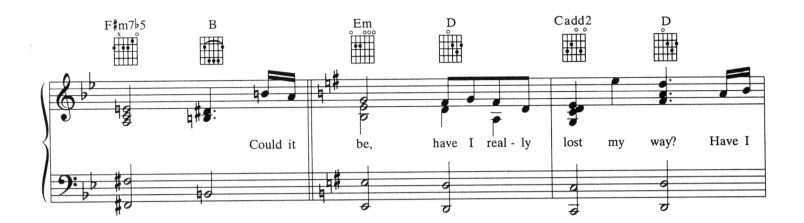

Could it be, have I real-ly lost my way? Have I

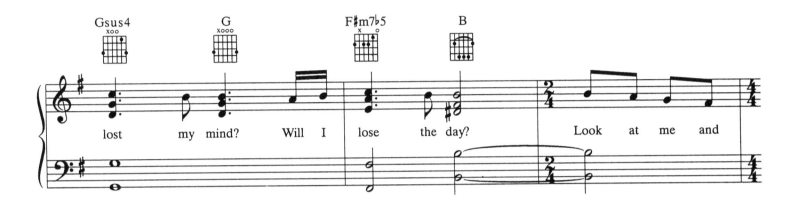

lost my mind? Will I lose the day? Look at me and

say where it all went wrong. This has been my dream my whole life

long. Those who dare to try, those who want to fly, will find a

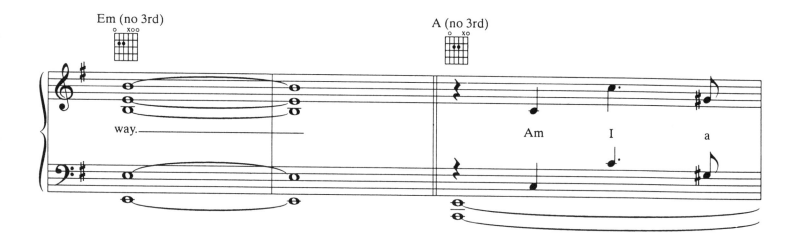

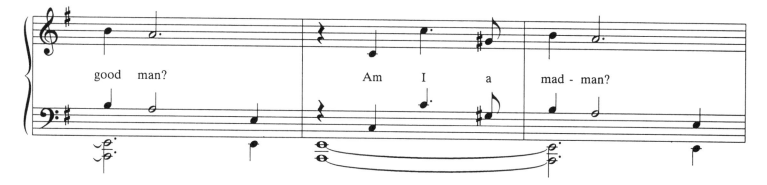

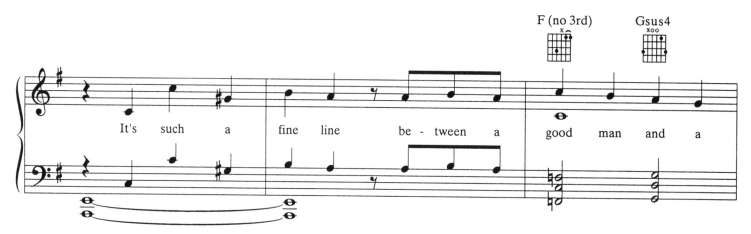

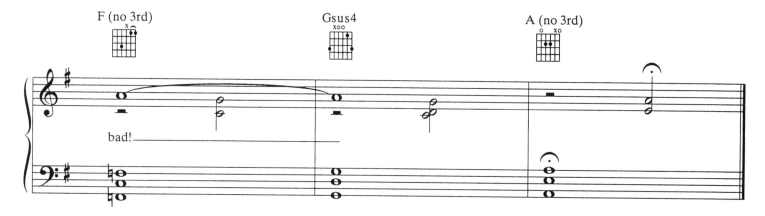

Possessed

Words by
Leslie Bricusse and Frank Wildhorn

Music by Frank Wildhorn

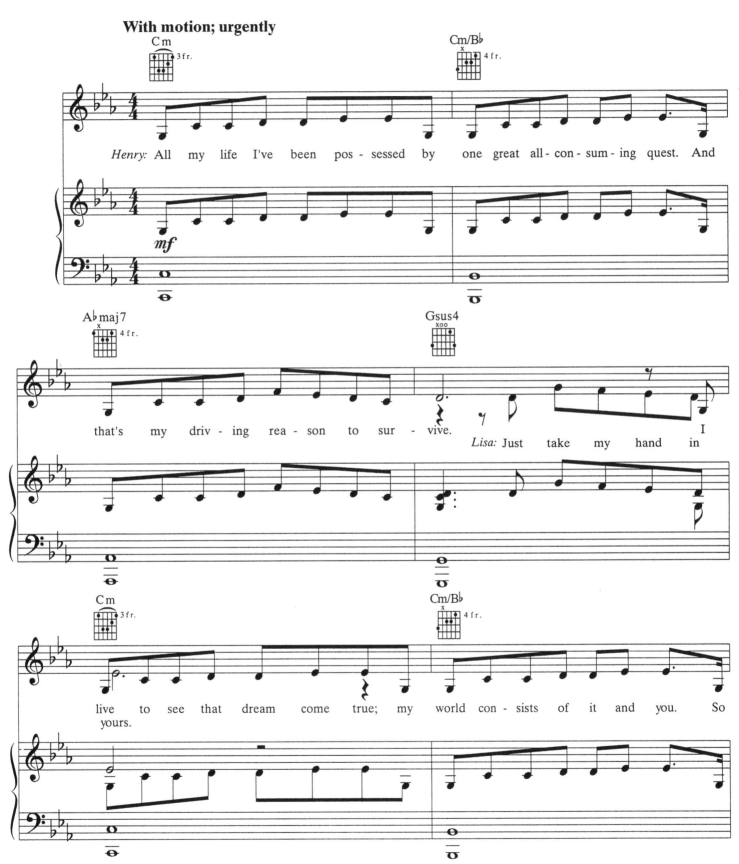

I have got to keep that dream a - live.

Lisa: Hen - ry, I a -

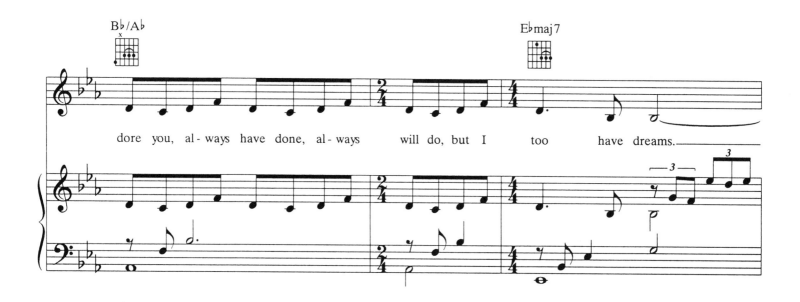

dore you, al - ways have done, al - ways will do, but I too have dreams.

May-be not as grand as yours, or hard to un-der-stand as yours, but

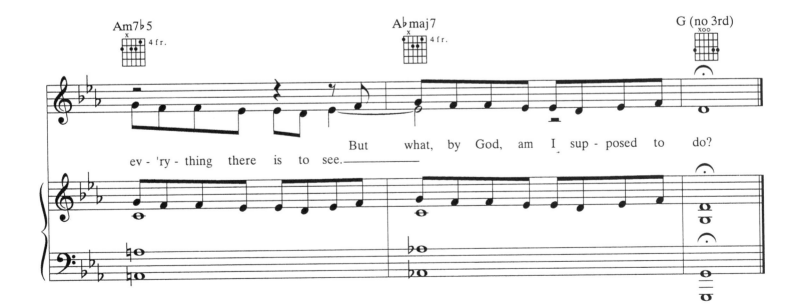

Retribution

Words by
Leslie Bricusse and Frank Wildhorn

Music by Frank Wildhorn

Moderately

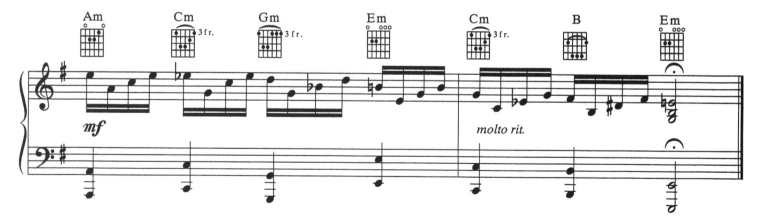

Seduction

Words by
Leslie Bricusse and Frank Wildhorn

Music by Frank Wildhorn

Flowing, expressive

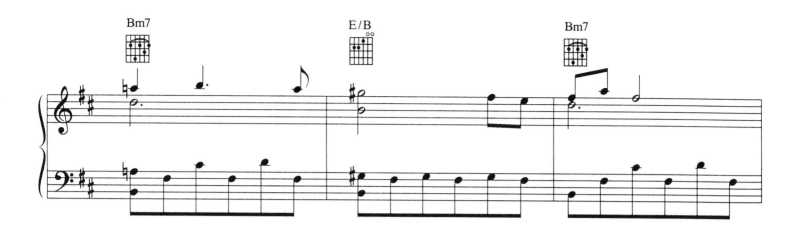

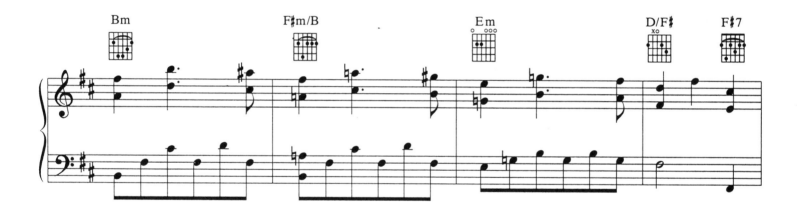

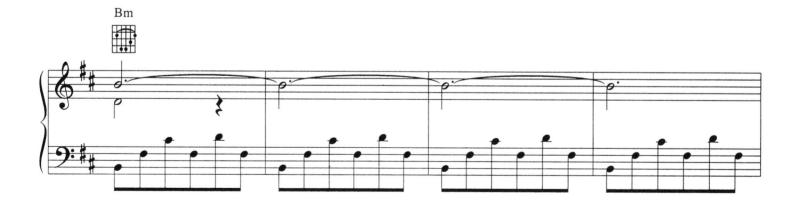

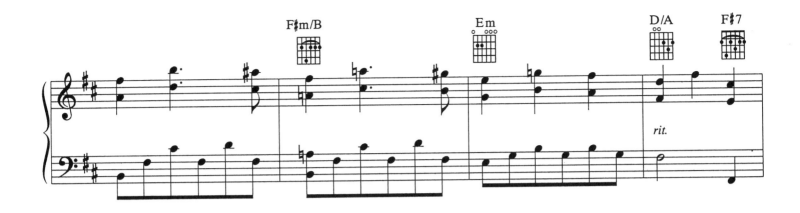

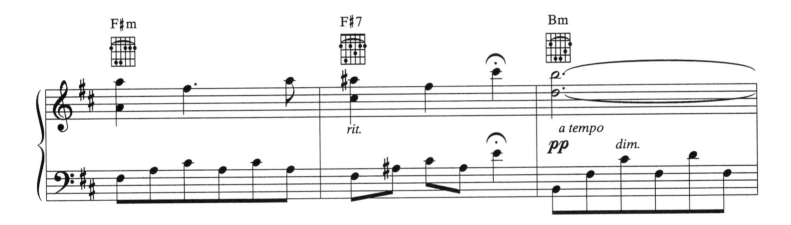

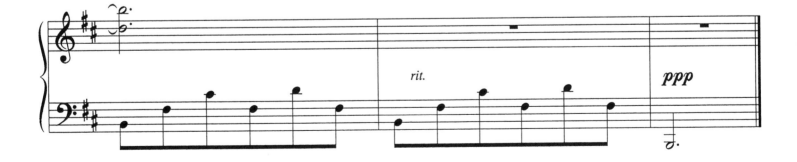

Till You Came into My Life

Words by Leslie Bricusse

Music by Frank Wildhorn

Moderately slow

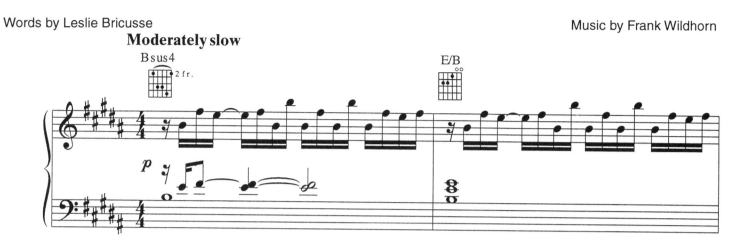

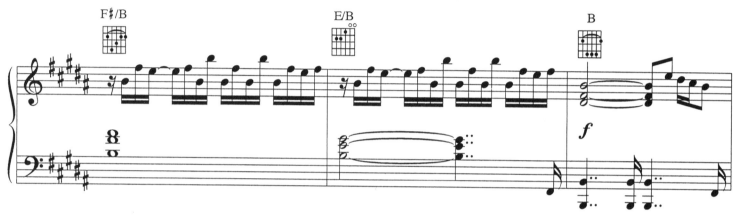

All my life
In your eyes

I've been build-ing walls a-round
I could lose my-self for-ev-

me,
er.   in my world   safe where no one's— ev - er
                   In your eyes   there's ex - cite - ment,— there is

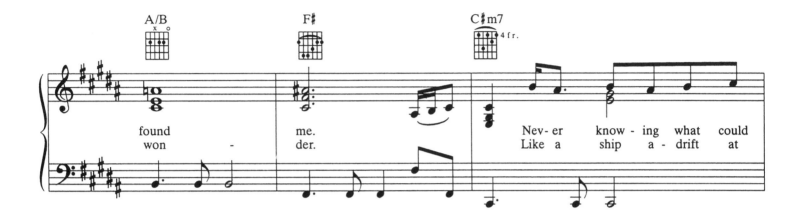

found   Nev - er   know - ing   what   could
won —   der.   Like a   ship   a - drift   at

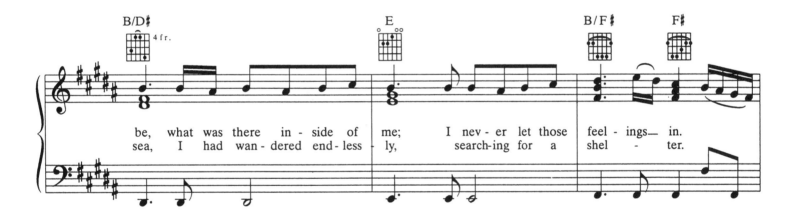

be,   what was there in - side of me;   I   nev - er let those   feel - ings— in.
sea,   I   had wan - dered end - less - ly,   search - ing for a   shel —ter.

Then up - on a sum - mer's night, you   gent - ly changed my life.   I would nev - er
Like a sweet im - a - gined dream, you were heav - en - sent to me;   you gave my   heart a

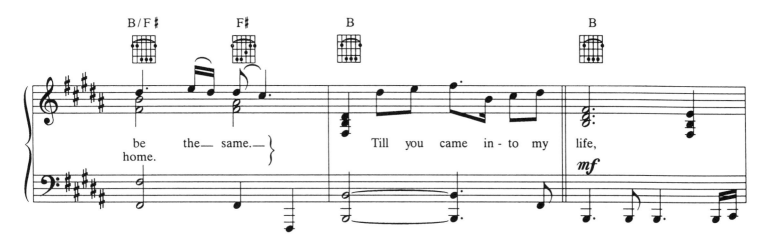

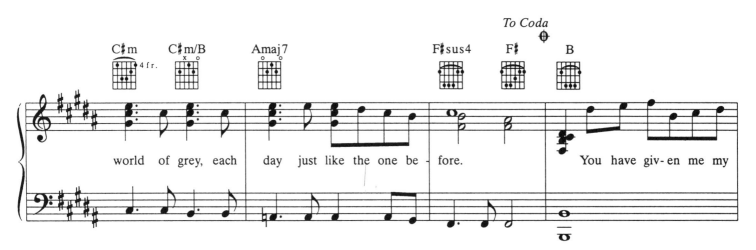

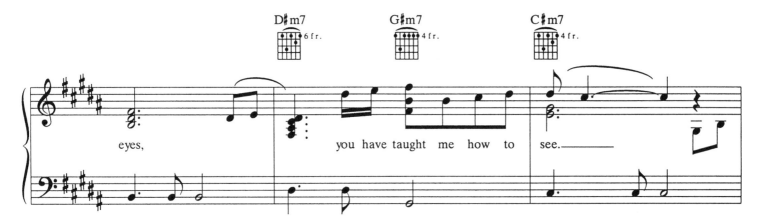

And now I see a brand-new world I nev-er dreamed could

be, till you came in-to my life.

D.S. al Coda

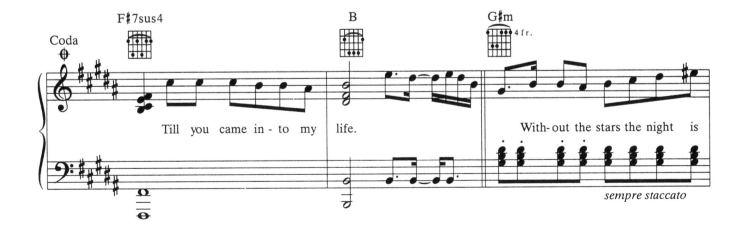

Till you came in-to my life. With-out the stars the night is

sempre staccato

em - pty;___ I was___ till there___ was you.___

Now you're the light that shines with - in me,___ guid - ing me

through._____ Till you came in - to my life,

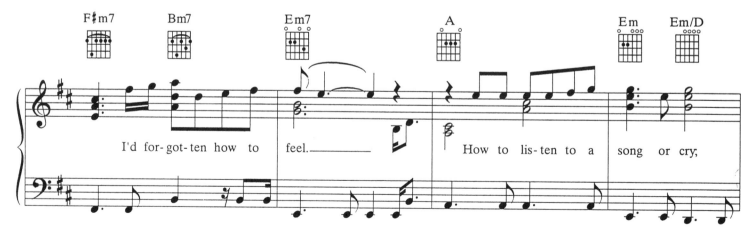

I'd for-got-ten how to feel._____ How to lis-ten to a song or cry;

64

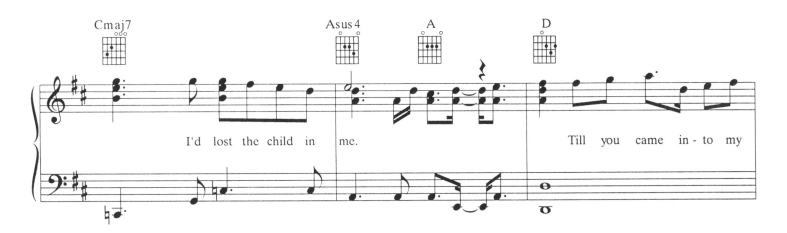

I'd lost the child in me. Till you came in-to my

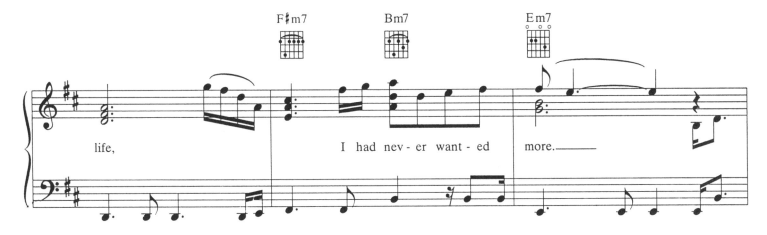

life, I had nev-er want-ed more.

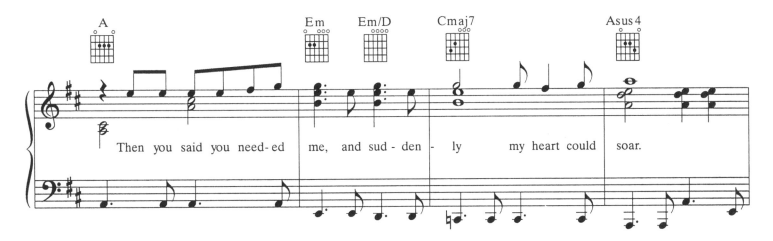

Then you said you need-ed me, and sud-den-ly my heart could soar.

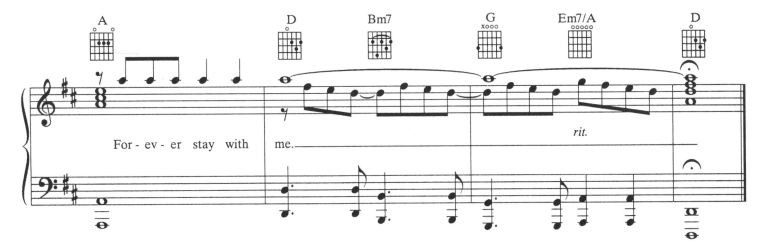

For-ev-er stay with me.

Transformation

Words by Steve Cuden,
Leslie Bricusse and Frank Wildhorn

Music by Frank Wildhorn

eyes? Now that it is done, there's noth-ing left to do, on-ly time can

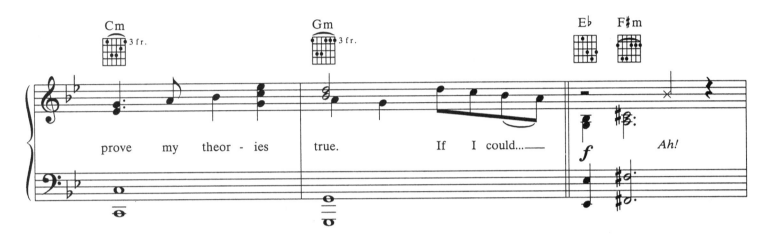

prove my theor-ies true. If I could..... *Ah!*

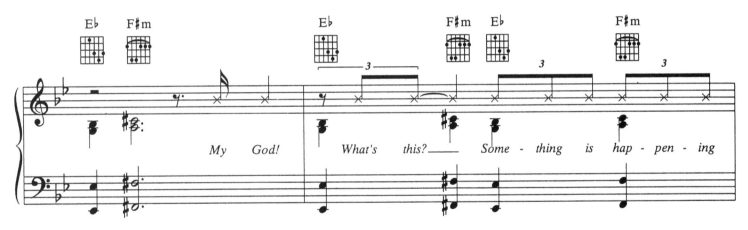

My God! What's this? Some - thing is hap - pen - ing

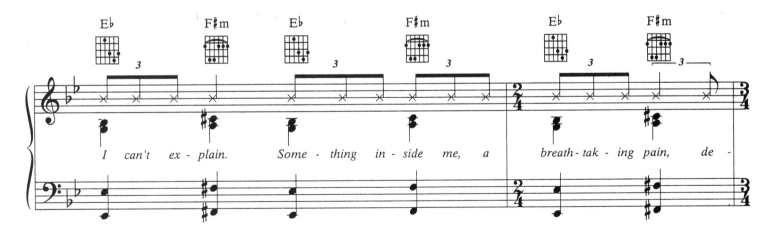

I can't ex - plain. Some - thing in - side me, a breath - tak - ing pain, de -

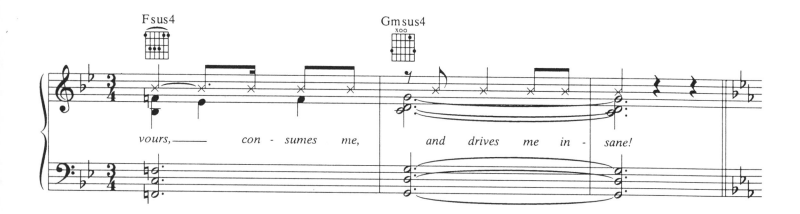

vours, _____ con - sumes me, and drives me in - sane!

Moderate waltz

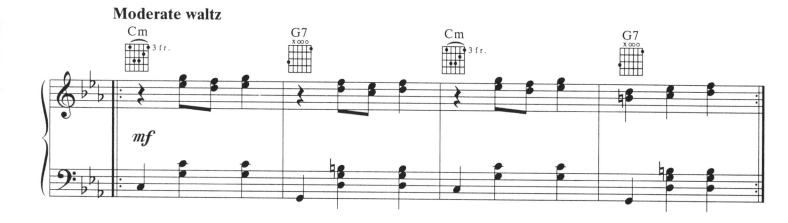

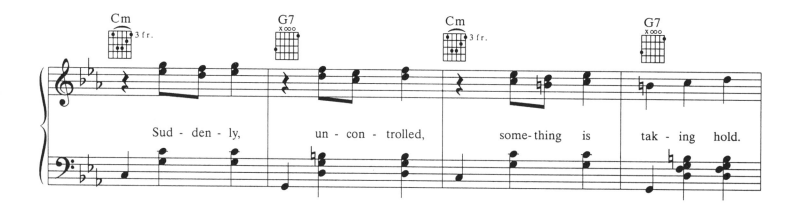

Sud - den - ly, un - con - trolled, some - thing is tak - ing hold.

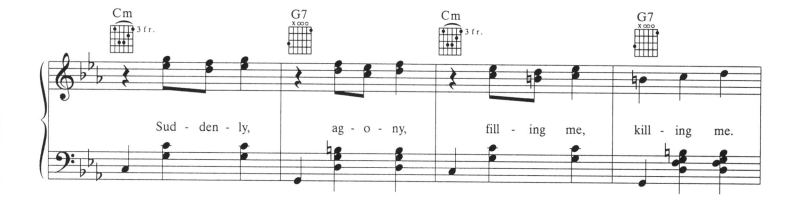

Sud - den - ly, ag - o - ny, fill - ing me, kill - ing me.

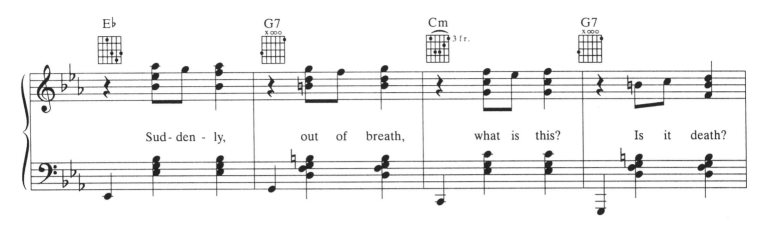

Sud - den - ly, out of breath, what is this? Is it death?

Slowly

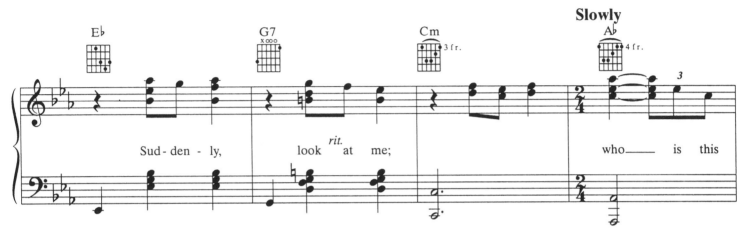

Sud - den - ly, look *rit.* at me; who____ is this

Tempo I

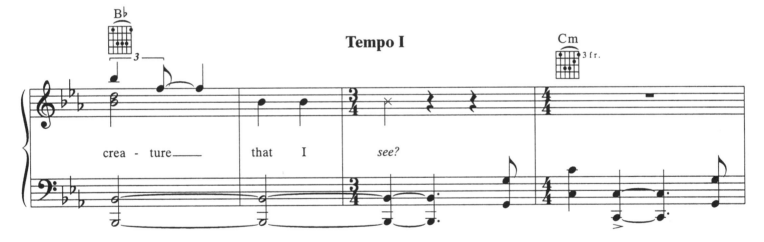

crea - ture____ that I *see?*

Repeat and fade

We Still Have Time

Words by Leslie Bricusse

Music by Frank Wildhorn

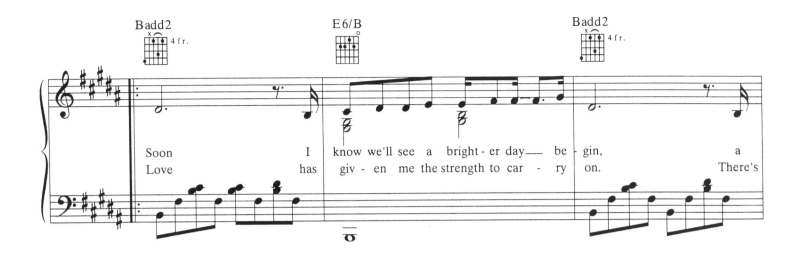

Soon I know we'll see a bright-er day— be - gin, a
Love has giv-en me the strength to car - ry on. There's

bet - ter and a wis-er world for liv - ing in, that we will share;
noth-ing I can't do as long as you are near, so close, my dear,

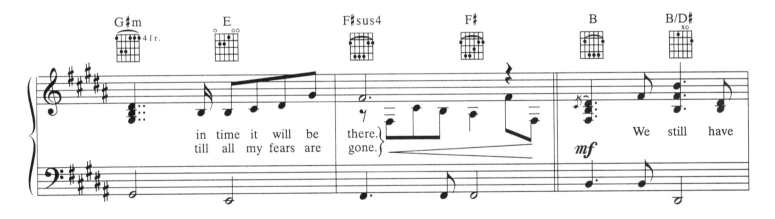

in time it will be there.) We still have
till all my fears are gone.) mf

time, we still can dream.

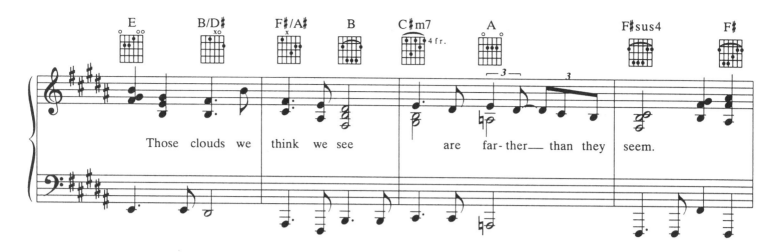

Those clouds we think we see are far-ther— than they seem.

We still have time, it's nev - er too

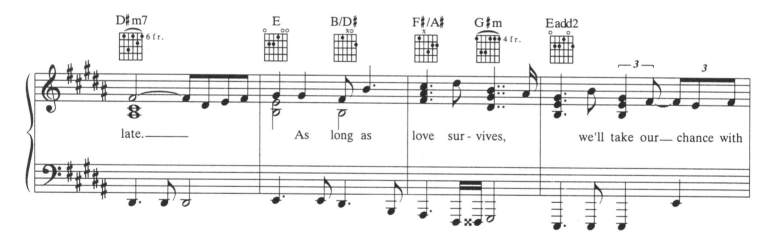

late.___ As long as love sur - vives, we'll take our— chance with

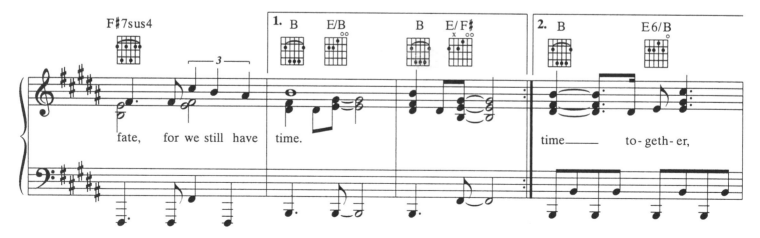

fate, for we still have time.

time___ to - geth - er,

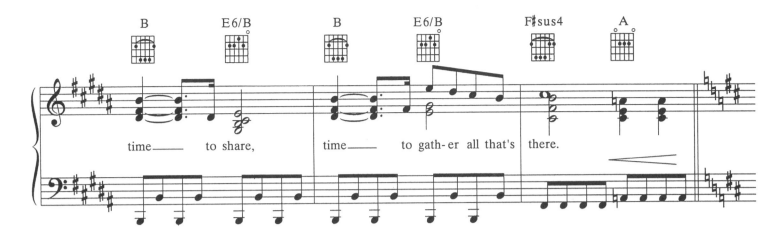

time —— to share, time —— to gath-er all that's there.

We still have time, it's nev-er too late.

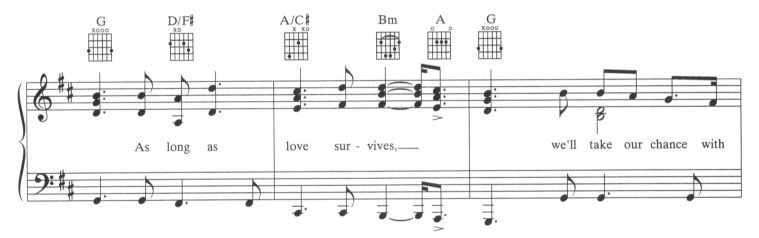

As long as love sur - vives, —— we'll take our chance with

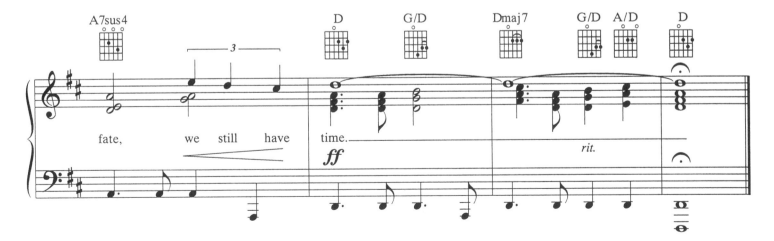

fate, we still have time.

The World Has Gone Insane

Words by Leslie Bricusse

Music by Frank Wildhorn

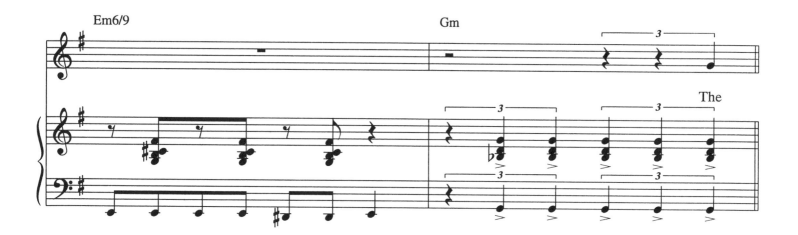

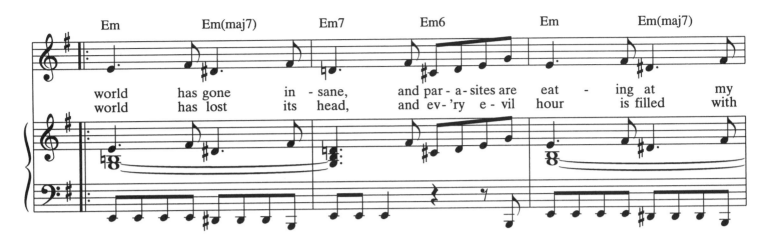

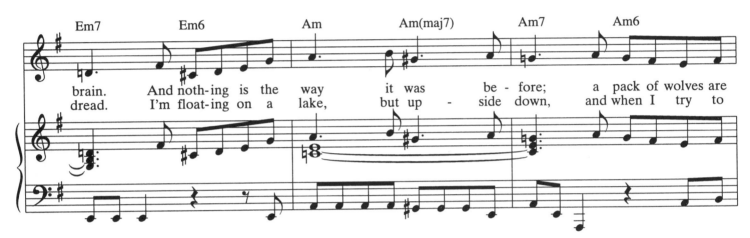

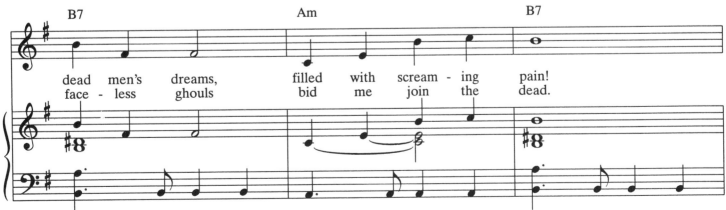

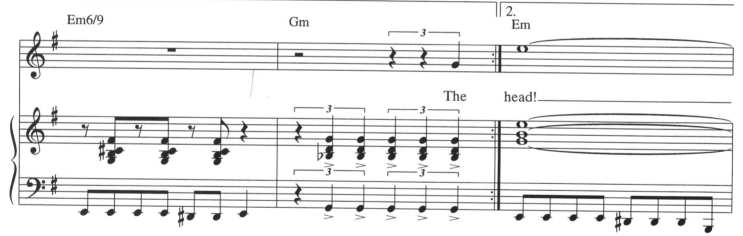

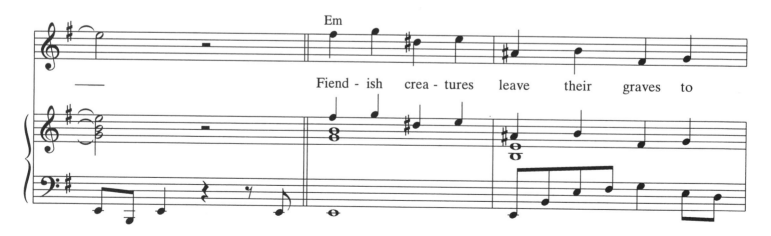

taunt me,_____ old friends ris - en

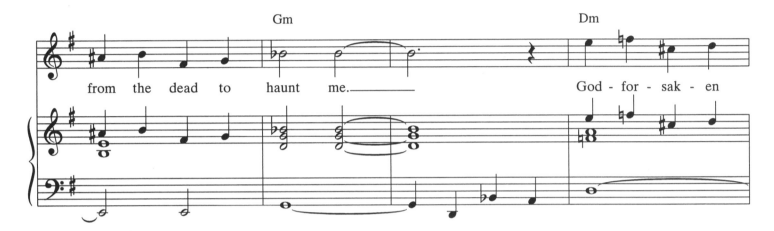

from the dead to haunt me._____ God - for - sak - en

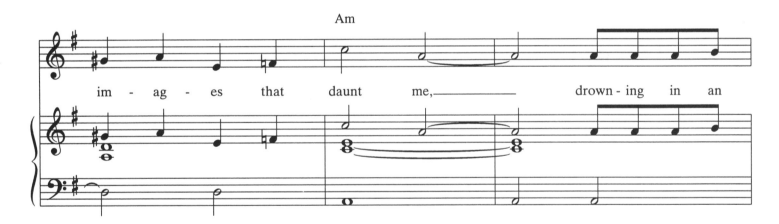

im - ag - es that daunt me,_____ drown - ing in an

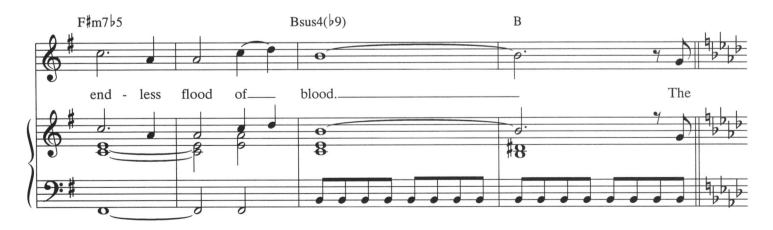

end - less flood of___ blood._____ The

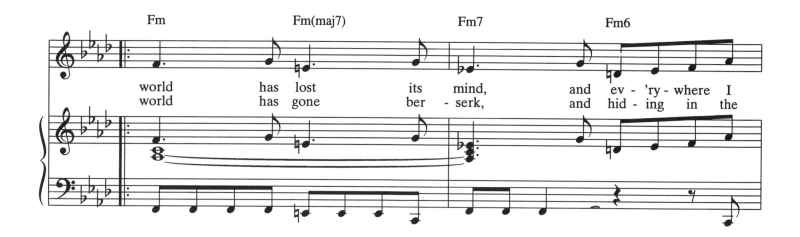

world has lost its mind, and ev-'ry-where I
world has gone ber - serk, and hid-ing in the

turn I fear I'll find some night-mare e - ven worse than those I
murk new mon - sters lurk. I see a sea of snakes up - on the

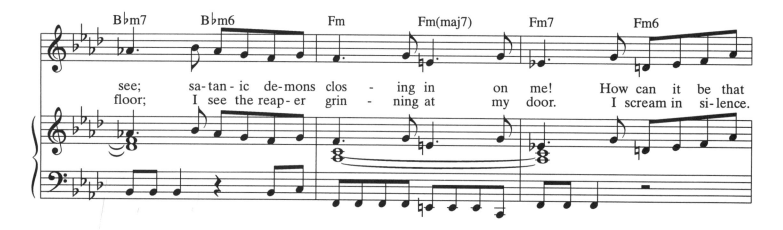

see; sa-tan-ic de-mons clos - ing in on me! How can it be that
floor; I see the reap-er grin - ning at my door. I scream in si-lence.

e - ven though they see my plight, ev-'ry-one is
Bad is good and good is bad; sa - cred is pro -

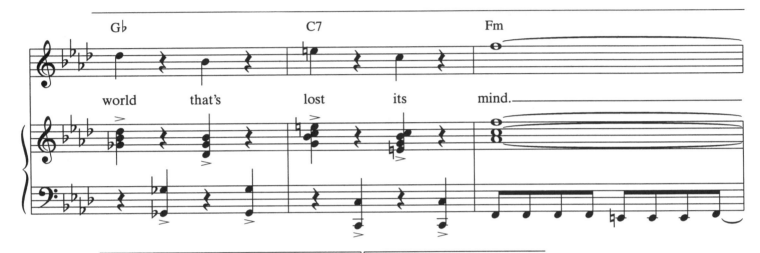